**WITHDRAWN
UTSA Libraries**

Eyewitness Accounts of the American Revolution

Memoir of Lieut. Col. Tench Tilghman

The New York Times & Arno Press

Reprinted from a copy in
The Pennsylvania State Library

*

Reprint Edition 1971 by Arno Press Inc.

*

LC# 79-140884
ISBN 0-405-01210-1

*

Eyewitness Accounts of the American Revolution, Series III
ISBN for complete set: 0-405-01187-3

*

Manufactured in the United States of America

MEMOIR

OF

LIEUT. COL. TENCH TILGHMAN

MEMOIR

OF

LIEUT. COL. TENCH TILGHMAN,

SECRETARY AND AID TO WASHINGTON,

TOGETHER WITH

AN APPENDIX,

CONTAINING

REVOLUTIONARY JOURNALS AND LETTERS, HITHERTO UNPUBLISHED.

Gloria Majorum, Lumen Posteris.

ALBANY:
J. MUNSELL, 82 STATE STREET.
1876.

Entered according to Act of Congress in the year 1876,
BY OSWALD TILGHMAN,
In the office of the Librarian of Congress.

As it was expected this Memoir would find most of its readers among the kinsmen of its subject, their connections and friends, pardon will be extended to the introduction of many details respecting his family, and local references, which have an interest for those only who are within this comparatively restricted circle.

No attempt has been made towards any formal editing of the Appendix. The journals and letters are printed simply as interesting memorials of our heroic age, and not as elucidating any obscure matter in our history. It is proper to say that the writer of the Memoir is in no way responsible for the contents of the Appendix, nor for the manner of their presentation.

June, 1876.

MEMOIR

OF

LIEUT. COL. TENCH TILGHMAN.

EMORIES of her most worthy citizens are the best wealth of the state. That people is poor indeed, that has never possessed such treasures; but poorer still that having had, has lost them. No improvidence is comparable with that which permits the recollections of the distinguished great or good to be wasted by neglect, or consumed by time—to fade into obscurity or to be lost in entire oblivion. Mortifying as may be the confession, the citizen of Maryland is unable to deny that his state, in common with all those which custom calls the South, a term which happily has lost much of its significance, is in this regard obnoxious to reproach. He may not be willing to acknowledge that his state is insensible of gratitude for valuable service, or incapable of appreciating exemplary virtue; yet it is too true, that men who in almost every department of human effort have illustrated the history of this commonwealth, or shall illustrate it when that history shall be worthily written; men who have wrought ably and thought wisely for the good of Maryland, as well under the limitations and restrictions of a colonial condition and a proprietary rule, as in the greater freedom and with the wider scope of state and national independence; that such men have been almost as completely forgotten, when the generation to which they belonged had passed away, as though they had lived in the heroic age of a Grecian or Roman antiquity. If their memories have been preserved at all in any degree of freshness, they have been perpetuated by the respectful veneration of their immediate descendants; or, more frequently, by a pride of birth, which cannot be wholly condemned, that seeks its justification, even when all else is lost, in tracing an origin to a reputable, and perhaps distinguished ancestry. The historian or annalist of Maryland, in his attempts to recover the lost lineaments of those lives which once blessed with their benefits or adorned with their graces his native state, looks in vain through the long galleries of literary portraiture, drawn by reverent or grateful hands, for the "counterfeit presentments" of Maryland's notable men. There he finds delineated only the dead of other commonwealths; or, as if placed there by chance, and not by design, he may discover some meagre and colorless sketches, some biographical silhouettes, of a few worthies of that state whose great merits compelled the tribute of a stranger's pen or pencil. If he would find memorials of his own compatriots he must seek them, not upon the shelves of libraries groaning under their weight of "lives;" not in the archives of learned societies filled to repletion with their "memoirs;" nor even in the all embracing columns of the dictionaries of biography: but he must look for them, hid away among the musty rubbish of our offices of public record, or thrust into the dusty garrets or vermin-infested chests and drawers of our old and decaying family mansions. When found, if found at all, these memorials are seen to be obscured, mutilated, and for all useful purposes to the historian, destroyed — they are but relics that serve to minister to the superstition of ancestral worship. Others of the sisterhood of states have sought to give a perpetuity to the memory of their noble dead, by preserving recollections of them with all the spicery and cerements of literary embalmment. Maryland has consigned her worthies to the oblivious earth, to mingle their dust with that of the undistinguished many. If by chance some curious antiquary seeking historic relics of a shadowy past, or some patient genealogist tracing the dubious thread of a long lost pedigree, or some more sordid searcher for defective titles to ancestral acres long since alienated, should in turning over the records in our public offices or parish vestries, discover evidences of the former existence, in our midst, of men who had filled the highest civic stations in the commonwealth with dignity and usefulness, or given lustre to her army in war, his surprise is like that of the rustic who turns up with his spade the fossil bones of some huge animal of a former age.[1] It is the object of this memoir to

---

[1] The indifference of Marylanders to the perpetuation of the memories of their distinguished fellow citizens has a most striking illustration at the

attempt the recovery from the obscurity of neglect, where they have lain for nearly one hundred years, like an antique statue covered with the debris of centuries, the lineaments that marked the character, and the incidents that clothed the life of a good, a wise, and a brave man, to whom Maryland gave parentage, birth, career and sepulture. In this attempt to revive, and perchance perpetuate his memory, in some degree will be removed, it is hoped, the reproach which adheres to his native state of forgetfulness of the deeds and indifference to the fame of her sons, and Maryland be admonished, when she shall call her roll of honor, with all her sister states, in this centennial year, to add one other name to the already long and lengthening list of her noble dead — the name of Tench Tilghman.

"Scribe tui gregis hunc, et fortem crede bonumque."

TENCH TILGHMAN, was born on the 25th of December, in the year 1744, at Fausley, the plantation of his father situated upon Fausley creek, a branch of St. Michael's river in the county of Talbot, Maryland,[1]

---

date of this writing, when, in view of the approaching centennial anniversary of American Independence, an attempt is making to procure the preparation of memoirs of all those who served the state in the early, or continental congresses. To many whose coöperation was solicited in this laudable and most pious work, the very names of these patriots and statesmen which were in all mens' mouths, at a momentous period in our history, were almost as new as those of the Assyrian kings that lately have been deciphered upon the earthen tablets exhumed from the palaces of ancient Babylonia. Biographers have to this date not been found willing to undertake the almost hopeless task of recovering and recording the incidents of their several careers.

[1] The farm belongs, in part to Mrs. Henry May, and in part to the author of this memoir.

about two miles from the town of Easton. He was of one of the most respectable families of the province. Richard Tilghman, surgeon, emigrated from the county of Kent, England, in or about the year 1662, settling first upon Canterbury Manor, of which he was the original patentee, upon Third Haven river in Talbot. Thence he removed, after a short time, to the Hermitage upon Chester river, then in Kent now in the county of Queen Anne's. This Richard Tilghman, was the grandfather of James Tilghman, the father of the subject of this memoir, and a lawyer by profession, who after removing from Talbot to Chestertown, in Kent, thence removed to Philadelphia in the year 1762. He was well known to the profession in Pennsylvania, where he became secretary to the Proprietary Land office, which department of the government " by the accuracy of his mind and the steadiness of his purpose he brought into a system as much remarked for order and equity as, from its early defects, it threatened to be otherwise."[1] He was one of the commissioners for the province of Pennsylvania, appointed, by Governor Penn, for settling the boundary line between the colonies and the Indian territory, held at Fort Stanwix in October and November 1768. He was also a member of the governor's council, and private secretary of Julianna, the widow of the late proprietary. In the dispute between the colonies and the mother country, he espoused the cause of the latter. The adoption of the principles of a loyalist involved the resignation of his public trusts and the loss of his

---

[1] Eulogium upon the Hon. Will. Tilghman, by Horace Binney, Esq.

private business, so that not long after the outbreak of hostilities he returned to Chestertown in Maryland, where he spent the remainder of his days. Such was his moderation and discretion, that, although his opinions were obnoxious, he enjoyed the respect of his fellow citizens, and received the considerate notice of Washington himself. It may be interesting to those who are fond of tracing the hereditary transmission of mental qualities, to state, that the wife of Mr. James Tilghman, and the mother of Tench Tilghman, was the daughter of Tench Francis, Esquire, the elder, originally of Ireland, from which he emigrated when a boy to Talbot county in Maryland, where he married, under romantic circumstances, the daughter of Foster Turbutt of Ottwell in that county, became clerk of the court and deputy commissary general. He removed to Philadelphia, where he became attorney general of the province of Pennsylvania, and rose to great eminence as a lawyer. He was the brother of Richard Francis, the author of a work entitled *Maxims of Equity,* and also brother of Dr. Philip Francis, the translator of Horace, who was the father of Sir Philip Francis the putative author of *Junius's Letters*.

Tench Tilghman was one of a family of twelve children. Of these six were brothers, he being the eldest, all of whom became men of good repute in their several positions, and some eminently distinguished. The second brother was Richard, who was educated as a lawyer at the Temple, in London, going abroad in the ship which conveyed Governor Eden of Maryland. He obtained employment in the civil service of the East India Company, under Warner

Hastings of whom he was the friend, and by whom he was recommended to the directory for the post of attorney general of India; but he died at sea, when returning from the East, before receiving the promised honor. The third brother was James Tilghman, also a lawyer by education, who settling in Maryland became, after the reform of the judiciary system of that state in 1790, one of the associate justices of the court for Talbot county, a kinsman of the same name being the chief judge. The fourth brother was the Hon. William Tilghman, for many years chief justice of Pennsylvania, a character as admirable as ever adorned the bench, if we may trust the words of one who knew him well, and who was every way capable of estimating his intellectual abilities and moral worth, the Hon. Horace Binney, who in an eulogy of unsurpassed eloquence has commemorated his achievements in law, and his private virtues. The fifth brother was Philemon Tilghman, who, in politics sympathizing with his father, at the early age of fifteen went to England, entered the British navy, in which he received a commission, and further connected himself with that service by marrying the daughter of Admiral Millbanke. The youngest brother was Thomas Ringgold Tilghman, a well known merchant, first of Alexandria and then of Baltimore, a man of great probity, but dying early rose to no prominence. The sisters were married to gentlemen of the first respectability upon the eastern shore of Maryland.[1]

---

[1] The authorities for these details are family memoranda and the Eulogium, by the Hon. Horace Binney, of the Hon. Judge W. Tilghman.

Of the early education of Tench Tilghman, the eldest of the brothers, little authentic information has been transmitted. He probably received his rudiments at some of the schools in Easton, near to which town he lived. There is a tradition that he was subsequently instructed by the Rev. John Gordon, rector of St. Michael's parish, a gentleman of attainments. At an early age, however, possibly before the removal of his father to Philadelphia in 1762, his maternal grandfather Tench Francis, for whom he was named, assumed the direction of his education, and he then obtained the instruction of the best masters, and the advantages of the best schools. His letters and other writings, which remain in the hand of his family, evince literary acquirements of no mean order, and a taste which is really admirable.

The advice of his grandfather, who had assumed as well the direction of his education as the care of his fortunes in life, supported as it was by the approbation of his father and his own inclinations, determined him in the selection of his calling and career. At a proper age, therefore, and doubtless after a proper apprenticeship, he connected himself with his uncle, Tench Francis, the younger of the name, and earnestly engaged in commercial pursuits in Philadelphia. This business connection, although of short duration, seems to have been attended with gratifying results as regards his fortune, for in a letter written years after, he states that it enabled him to accumulate, before its dissolution in 1775, a moderate competency. A business which was commenced under the most favorable auspices and which had been conducted with so much success, was destined very soon to be destroyed, not through any lack of judgment or of prudence, but by the breaking of the political storm of the American revolution, which shipwrecked so many mercantile adventures. The manner in which Mr. Tilghman acted in the emergency evinces the man of honor, who scorns to take advantage of public disturbances and the suspension of law, for his own benefit. But an account of his conduct is best given in his own language. "Upon the breaking out of the troubles, I came to a determination to share the fate of my country; and that I might not be merely a spectator, I made as hasty a close, as I possibly could, of my commercial affairs, making it a point to collect and deposit in safe hands, as much as would, when times and circumstances would permit, enable me to discharge my European debts, which indeed were all I had, except £—— put in my hands by Mr. R., sen., in trust for my youngest brother: but as security for that I left, and have yet, a much larger sum in my father's hands. After I had happily collected and deposited the sum first mentioned, my outstanding debts began to be paid in depreciated money; and as I never took the advantage of a single penny in that way, I have sorely felt the pernicious effect of *tender* laws."[1] What is here related to one who had every opportunity of knowing the truth of every incident, is nothing more than might have been expected of a man of such scrupulous integrity, a feature in his character universally and at all times recognized.

---

[1] See letter to Matthew Tilghman, in appendix.

But disappointed as Mr. Tilghman was in his cherished hopes of realizing wealth, apprehensive as he must have been, from the first, that what little he had accumulated would be swept away in the cataclysm which was upon the country, all these painful emotions were scarcely felt in that exaltation of patriotic sentiment which he shared in common with his fellow citizens. The battles of Lexington and Concord had been fought. The whole country was aflame. Even Philadelphia, the characteristic features of whose population, then more than now, were a quietude and calmness inherited from a Quaker origin, was aroused to the manifestation of military ardor. Volunteer military associations were formed, which the peaceful principles of the Friends did not prevent the more ardent of their young men from joining, and which the chivalrous spirit of those of other faiths and parentage gladly adopted. With one of these organizations Mr. Tilghman connected himself. The name which it assumed, as well as that by which it was derisively designated by those disaffected to the patriot cause, indicates the character of the materials of which this company was composed. It was called "The Ladies Light Infantry," by those who thought well of the company and its objects; but it was named "The Silk Stockings," by tories and those who placed a low estimate upon its military efficiency. It was commanded by a scion of one of the most respectable and prominent of Maryland families, Captain Sharpe Dulaney, and was composed of the *jeunesse doré* of the city of Philadelphia—of young men of the best social position. In this company Tench Tilghman, another Marylander, and as well born as his superior officer, was lieutenant. As a part of the forces contributed by Pennsylvania, this body, or one into which it merged, with Tilghman, however, as captain, joined the army of Washington. This connection of Mr. Tilghman, with a volunteer company of Pennsylvania militia, which promised only danger and hardship, with little distinction or reward, opened the path by which he attained a position of honor and responsibility in the army of the United States, and the friendship of the peerless man.

While thus surrendering himself to the impulses of patriotism, he was violating some of the tenderest sentiments of his nature. Trained up in a filial piety towards his parents, more common in the past than now; accustomed from his youth to respect the desires and opinions of one whose character as well as his relation entitled him to the reverence of a son; he found himself impelled by a sense of higher duty than that he owed to his father to disregard his wishes and to depart from his advice. Mr. James Tilghman, as has before been mentioned, adhered to the crown, conscientiously believing, as did many of the most worthy citizens in all the colonies, that the maintenance of the royal authority, and a continuance of the connection with the mother country, were the part of true patriotism and of a wise policy. When the crisis came, Mr. Tench Tilghman found himself at variance with his honored father; but it would appear from the correspondence which was maintained between them during the whole war, that differences of opinion upon political subjects never produced any alienation of feeling, and that a mutual affection and respect was cherished to the end. To be sure the persistence of the father in unfavorable and tantalizing comments upon the course of congress, and his depreciatory reflections upon the strength and the behavior of the patriot army, sometimes caused a momentary impatience in the son, who was serving under that congress and in that army, and caused him to ask with some warmth, not only on the ground of prudence but for the sake of good feeling, that there should be no farther political discussions in the letters that should pass between them;[1] but even under this provocation there is no word that is not consistent with that honor and respect which it was his wish to render to him to whom they were due. Col. Tilghman frequently in his letters to his father expressed a solicitude that he would consent to take the oath to the existing government of Pennsylvania which had been prescribed; using the argument that there would be no inconsistency between the position he had taken in the beginning of the troubles, and that which he would

---

[1] In a letter dated Feb. 22, 1777, to his father he says: "I know we do not agree in political sentiments, quite, but that, I am convinced, does not abate, in the least, that ardent affection which I have for you, and which makes me happy, far happier than any other title when I call myself, your most dutiful son."

In a letter dated April 21, 1777, he says: "I late last night recd. yours of 21st. The contents really make me exceedingly unhappy, as I find myself unable to agree with you in sentiment upon the present measures. * * * I will say nothing upon the score of politics, because it is a subject that ought not at this time to be discussed upon paper. I wish it might be dropped in all future letters between us."

hold after submitting to the established order of things, which he not only had no part in forming, but had resisted while it was forming, and then was powerless to overthrow. He also mentioned, by way of inducing his father to take the step, a number of loyalists of social prominence who had already taken the oath, and others who were about to accept it. Another source of disquietude to Col. Tench Tilghman, as well as to his father, which may be mentioned in this connection, was the conduct of a young brother, Mr. Philemon Tilghman, who had left his home at the early age of fifteen years and connected himself with the British naval forces then operating against the United States. The father and brother were equally anxious to secure the return of this impulsive youth, both feeling that his prospects in life had been destroyed; the father seeing no hope of promotion and advancement in a service where he had no influential friends, the brother perceiving that he had completely shut himself off from a career in America.[1] Mr. James Tilghman occasionally communicated with Mr. Philemon Tilghman, through Col. Tilghman, who sent his letters by a flag of truce, when there was communication between head quarters and the fleet. It would seem from a letter to another brother, Mr. William Tilghman, who had written to him asking that he would procure for him permission to go to England,

---

[1] In a letter dated Feb. 27, 1778, Col. T. says: "His first act was a boyish trick, and might have been overlooked. But thank God he has chosen a service that will never throw him in my way as an enemy. I will endeavor to forward a letter to him, if you will send it to me."

for the purpose of prosecuting his law studies, that attempts had been made to arouse suspicion in Gen. Washington's mind against his secretary, founded upon his family connection with many persons who were disaffected to the patriot cause, to whom he had rendered service. In this letter he says : " It gives me pain to tell you that I cannot, without subjecting myself to censure, interfere in the least, in procuring you recommendations to go to England, by way of France and Holland. I am placed in as delicate a situation as it is possible for a man to be. I am, from my station, master of the most valuable secrets of the cabinet and the field, and it might give cause of umbrage and suspicion were I, at this critical moment (June 12, 1781), to interest myself in procuring the passage of a brother to England. Tho' I know his intentions are perfectly innocent, others may not, or will not. You cannot conceive how many attempts have been made, some time ago, to alarm the general's suspicions as to my being near his person. Thank God — he has been too generous to listen to them, and the many proofs I have given of my attachment have silenced every malignant whisper of the kind. As I have never given the least handle for censure, I am determined never to do it."

Before Mr. Tilghman was called upon for active service in the field, for which he had been so prompt to offer himself, with a disregard of his pecuniary interests, his personal comfort and his family ties which only a sense of patriotic duty could inspire, he had the privilege of serving his country in a civil capacity. Already, in 1775, the more perspicacious of the statesmen who composed the congresses, meeting at Philadelphia, foresaw, what the bolder of them had determined to compel, a separation of the colonies from Great Britain, and the establishment of a distinct government or governments. Measures looking to the assumption and maintenance of an advanced position, with regard to colonial independence, were promptly taken soon after the shedding of blood in New England. Troops were ordered to be raised, a commander-in-chief, with subordinate officers, was appointed, stores and munitions were collected, and all other preparations incident to war were made with the utmost promptness and energy. The British forces in America came to be regarded as enemies, and the British government as hostile and alien, although a formal declaration of independence had not yet been promulgated. Besides these preparative measures of a warlike character, others of a precautionary kind were taken to secure peaceful neutrality or active alliance. Among these measures may be mentioned those which respected the protection of the frontiers from the incursions of the neighboring Indians. It was apprehended that the savages, who were then at peace, taking advantage of the embarrassments incident to war, would renew their depredations and hostilities upon the settlements of the unprotected border. The most serious trouble was anticipated from those tribes of the Iroquois, which had early formed a league under the name of the Six Nations. These tribes, although greatly diminished in numbers since the first settlements of the Europeans, and although they had partially adopted the habits of civilization, were still formidable enough to a struggling confederation of colonies. The danger was the more threatening in that it was known they were under English influence, and thus ready at the prompting of the British agent to fall upon any whom he might designate as enemies of the royal government and of themselves.

The memory of Sir William Johnson, the former superintendent of Indian affairs of the crown, who had died the year before, was still a potential influence among them. His cousin and son-in-law Guy Johnson, who succeeded him in his influence and in his office, was known to be inimical to the patriot cause, and to be already actively employed in enlisting these tribes whose seat was New York, and others in the adjoining provinces of Canada, against the United Colonies, as they now wished to be called. For the purpose of securing the neutrality of the Indians along the whole frontier, congress on the 13th July, 1775, appointed three commissions to form treaties: one for the Six Nations, and other tribes towards the north; a second for the Creeks or Cherokees towards the south; and a third for the intervening tribes towards the west. The gentlemen who were chosen commissioners for the northern department were Major General Philip Schuyler, Major Joseph Hawley, Mr. Turbutt Francis, Mr. Oliver Wolcott, and Mr. Volckert P. Douw. The commissioners were vested with " powers to treat with the Indians in their respective departments, to preserve peace and friendship, and to prevent their taking part in the present commotion.[1] A speech to the six confederate nations, Mohawks, Oneidas, Tuscaroras, Onondagas, Cayugas, and Senecas, from the twelve United Colonies, convened in council at Philadelphia, was framed to be read at the assembly of the tribes, and an appropriation of seven hundred and fifty dollars was made to entertain the sachems and warriors of the Six Nations, when they should come to Albany and Schenectady. With this commission Mr. Tilghman, doubtless through the influence of his maternal uncle, Mr. Turbutt Francis, one of the members chosen by congress, was connected in the capacity of secretary and treasurer or paymaster. A report was made in due form to congress, of the proceedings of the commission, the preparation of which, there is good ground to believe, was the work of Mr. Tilghman. This report is published in the American Archives, and elsewhere, and makes up a part of the general history of the nation. But besides this official account, which was made for the information of congress, Col. Tilghman has left behind him a private journal, in which, while referring to the public acts of the commissioners, he gives many details that were not admissible in a paper designed for the inspection, information and guidance of the highest legislative body of the United Colonies. The period embraced in this diary of events, and record of personal experience, is from Aug. 5th, 1775, the date when the commissioners left New York, to Sept. 4th,

---

[1] New York Historical Society Collections, vol. VIII, p. 605.

of the same year, when they returned to that point. It is written with minuteness of detail, but, strange to say, fails to indicate the relation he held to the commission to which he was attached. It is the product evidently of a current pen, and prepared with no purpose that it should be published, though its correctness of expression, as well as nicety of mechanical execution, fits it for the press with small labor of revision or alteration. It was designed for the amusement of his brothers and sisters at home, and is addressed to his brother Richard. Of its literary execution it may be said that, written with haste, and under the disadvantages of the preoccupation incident to his position as secretary, and of the necessity of constant movement, it evinces that facility in the arts of expression which is acquired by most persons only after long and habitual use of the pen in composition, and that correctness of taste which no practice seems to confer, but which is the result of a natural sensibility to what is refined and pleasing. Apart from the value which the journal possesses, by reason of the relation it bears to an important event in the early revolutionary history, it is interesting as furnishing a very graphic account of the country and the towns through which he passed while in attendance on the commission, and a vivid and pleasing glimpse of social life at Albany and its vicinity. To the biographer, and those who wish to gain an insight into the character of the writer, this journal has this other value and interest; that it reveals a trait as rare as it is admirable — purity of mind: for though it is filled with banter, badinage and other light or trivial matter which one young man might be expected to write to another in the freedom of correspondence, and much of this, too, with reference to the other sex, not one word has escaped his pen which may not be read by the chastest eyes without offence. Indeed one single expression, which prudishness might pervert into something indelicate, he has erased, but not so effectually that curious eyes may not decipher the really harmless words. The following extract, of a purely personal nature, will serve at once to exhibit his familiar style of writing, and to present a curious incident which occurred during the treaty, but which is not recorded in the official report: "Thursday, Aug. 24. We dined this day with the General [Schuyler] who has a palace of a house, and lives like a prince. The ladies from Carolina [the Misses Lynch] the commissioners and several gentlemen from the neighboring provinces were there. Having occasion to meet some of the Indian chiefs in the evening, they asked if I had an Indian name. Being answered in the negative, Teahoga, the chief of the Onondagos, did me the honor to adopt me into the tribe, and to become my father. He christened me Teahokalonde, a name of very honorable signification among them, but much to the contrary among us. It signifies having large horns. A deer is the coat of arms, if I may call it, of the Onondago tribe, and they look upon horns as an emblem of strength, virtue and courage. * * * The christening cost a bowl of punch or two, which I believe was the chief motive of the institution. Friday, Aug. 26. The treaty was opened with great form. * * * When business was over, I was admitted to the Onondago tribe in presence of the Six Nations, and received by them as an adopted son. They told me that in order to settle myself among them they must choose me a wife, and promised she should be one of the handsomest they could find. I accepted the proposal with thanks. Miss Lynch and Miss Betsy Schuyler have promised to stand bridesmaids." Miss Schuyler to whom reference is made was the daughter of Gen. Philip Schuyler, and subsequently the wife of Gen. Alexander Hamilton, characters whom all the world knows. The commissioners were handsomely entertained at her father's house, while she seems to have interested herself to make the time of the secretary, whose years more nearly approached her own, pass pleasantly, which otherwise would have hung heavily on his hands while waiting the slow deliberations of the Indian council. Of this lady, who enjoyed in after years a brilliant social career, and late in life a nation's veneration, he speaks in his journal in such glowing terms that there is reason to suspect that a more tender sentiment than mere admiration was the origin of such ardor of praise. Other extracts from this diary might be made, but as they would serve in no special way further to illustrate the life of Col. Tilghman, they may be omitted, and the reader be referred to the journal itself, which is published entire in the appendix to this memoir.

It would thus appear that the first services which Mr. Tilghman was privileged to render to his country were in a civil capacity, humble, it is true, but honorable. He had already shown his readiness to serve as a soldier, by his uniting himself with the volunteer company of which Sharpe Dulaney was captain. Upon the requisition of congress upon the several colonies for troops, he was among the first to offer his service to the commonwealth of his adoption, and a company composed, doubtless, of many of the members of the Ladies Light Infantry, was accepted by Pennsylvania, with Tench Tilghman as captain. Of the precise date when this company was mustered in there has been discovered no record; but it is well known that in the early part of the year 1776, this company from Philadelphia joined the army of Washington, and made a part of what was called the Flying Camp. From some intimations contained in his letters it would seem that it was the purpose of Capt. Tilghman, originally, to serve one campaign, the most of the early troops having been mustered in for short terms; but his behavior in the service in which he was then engaged was such as to attract the attention of his superiors in rank. His own personal merits as shown in the field, his high social position, his liberal education, supported it is true by the recommendations of partial friends in Philadelphia, caused him to be invited to take a place upon the staff of the commander-in-chief, and this resulted in his continuance in the "barren military line," as he himself calls his service in the army, by way of contrast with the more profitable positions in civil or private life. It is well known that General Washington, during the first year of his command, had experienced much difficulty in securing the services of gentlemen of proper qualifications for filling the positions of aids and secretaries. His first appointments to these places were Cols. Mifflin and Trumbull as aids, and Col. Joseph Reed as secretary; but changes had been frequent at head quarters. In a letter addressed to Col. Robert H. Harrison — a Marylander — one of those secretaries, and the oldest, he said: "As for military knowledge, I do not find gentlemen much skilled in it. If they can write a good letter, write quick, are methodical and diligent, it is all I expect to find in my aids." But even of Col. Harrison, himself, he said: "Though sensible, clever, and perfectly confidential, he has never yet moved on so large a scale as to comprehend at one view the diversity of matter which comes before me, so as to afford that ready assistance which every man in my situation must stand more or less in need of.[1] These expressions indicate the qualifications of the person who should hold the responsible position and intimate relation of secretary to Washington; and they gave assurance that the man whom he should select to fill this place, after frequent trials and disappointments, and who should be able to retain the post during the continuance of the whole war, was the one who satisfied all the requisites. Such a man was Tench Tilghman. In August of 1776, he became a member of the military family of Washington, the other members at that time being Col. Robert. H. Harrison, Col. Mead, and Col. Webb — the last of

---

[1] Hamilton's *History of the Republic of the United States*, vol. I, p. 173.

whom, upon promotion gave place in 1777 to Col. Hamilton.[1]

Difficulties and disputes having arisen among the officers respecting the order of their promotion, congress having neglected to establish any principle of graduation of universal application, Gen. Washington, on the 11th May, 1781, from head quarters at New Windsor, addressed a letter to the Hon. John Sullivan, a delegate in that body, urging, with great earnestness, the adoption of some rule which should reconcile the disagreements and quiet the discontents which were keeping the army in a state of distraction. The whole of this letter is most important to the historian of the war, but that portion of it which relates to the subject of this memoir, and is here copied, is especially interesting to the biographer of Col. Tilghman, inasmuch as it not only elucidates some obscurities in his military career, but also, in narrating his devotion to duty, his fidelity to the cause, the unselfishness of his service and his generosity to his fellow-officers, it presents phases of his character admirable, if they may not be called even wonderful. "I also wish, though it is more a matter of private than of public consideration, that the business could be taken up on account of Mr. Tilghman, whose appointment seems to depend

---

[1] In speaking of this military family, of which he at one time formed a part, General Lafayette says: "during a familiar association of five years, that no instance of disagreement occurred, is evidence of the tone of feeling which prevailed."— Hamilton's *History of the Republic of the United States*, vol. I, p. 172.

Such concord could have been maintained only where there was mutual respect between the members, and where each was dominated by the same feeling of devotion to a common cause.

on it; for if there are men in the army deserving of the commission proposed for him, he is one of them. This gentleman came out a captain of one of the light infantry companies of Philadelphia, and served in the Flying Camp in 1776. In August of the same year he joined my family, and has been in every action in which the main army was concerned. He has been a zealous servant and slave to the public, and a faithful assistant to me for nearly five years, a great part of which time he refused to receive pay. Honor and gratitude interest me in his favor, and make me solicitous to obtain his commission. His modesty and love of concord placed the date of his expected commission at the first of April, 1777, because he would not take rank of Hamilton and Meade, who were declared aids in order (which he did not choose to be), before that period, although he had joined my family and done all the duties of one from the first of September preceding."[1] This letter, considering the source from which it emanated, the sentiments which it expressed, and the character of the actions which it indicated and commended, is as high an encomium as was ever bestowed upon any man. It would appear from this and other evidence, that although he entered upon the duties of secretary to Gen. Washington in August, 1776, and was from the September following discharging the functions of an aid-de-camp, with the title, by courtesy, of colonel, his rank had not been definitively established or declared. With an abnegation which is almost incredible, and a magnanimity

---

[1] Sparks's *Writings of Washington*, vol. VIII, p. 37.

Memoir of Lt. Col. Tench Tilghman.

almost beyond praise, in applying for his commission, instead of demanding that it should date from the time when he took position upon the staff, he consented that it should date from the first of April, 1777, that he might not outrank Colonels Hamilton and Meade, who had been recognized as aids, anterior to that period. It is felt that any comment upon this action, would be derogatory. Let it stand, therefore, in all its simple majesty and beauty. His commission was issued in accordance with his own wishes, and dating from 1st April, 1777, but issued May 30th, 1781.[1] The rank thus formally and authoritatively bestowed, as well as his position of assistant secretary to the commander-in-chief, he continued to hold until the close of the war, and the disbanding of the army, without seeking or desiring promotion. His ambition seemed to have been fully gratified by the possession of the confidence and approbation of his chief. There is a tradition, however, in the family, which has probability in its favor, that promotion was offered, but uniformly declined. This refusal may have been founded upon a consciousness of his own greater aptitude for the *quasi* civil duties of secretary at head quarters, than for independent military command; or, as is more probable, upon a very natural unwillingness to be separated, which promotion involved, from his honored commander, with whom his relations were of a more intimate kind than usually subsist between

---

[1] A copy of this commission may prove interesting to those who are not familiar with the form which had been adopted by the Board of War somewhat anterior to this date. It may be found in the appendix.

a superior and inferior officer, and for whom his attachment was stronger than such as could be severed by a simple dissolution of official connection.

To follow the career of Col. Tilghman during the war would be to write the whole history of the army under the immediate command of General Washington. In the letter already quoted, it is stated explicitly, " he has been in every action in which the main army was concerned." He was one of those who earliest embarked in the cause of independence, having been commissioned, probably in the year 1775, a captain of one of those independent companies which made up that body of troops called the Flying Camp. In that capacity he served until August, 1776, when he surrendered his captaincy for a place upon the personal staff of the commander-in-chief, as has been before stated. No record remains to indicate whether he participated in any of the operations of the army up to the latter date, though it is presumable that he did; but soon after this time, indeed immediately, he was called upon to take part in the disastrous battle of Long Island, and to share with Washington the mortification of the defeat which was there encountered, and his indignation at the conduct of some of the troops in the subsequent precipitate retreat from New York to Haarlem Heights.[1] In the successful affair at Manhattanville, which did so much to encourage the dis-

---

[1] In a letter to his father dated Aug. 13, 1776, he thus speaks of the Maryland troops in this action: " No regular troops ever made a more gallant resistance than Smallwood's regiment. If the others had behaved as well, if Gen. Howe had obtained a victory at all, it would have been dearly bought."

spirited army, history records his active participation. There, it is said, " he joined in the action to animate the troops, who charged with the greatest intrepidity."[1] Some of these troops that behaved so handsomely on this occasion were of his native Maryland. From this time onward, until he stood beside Washington at Annapolis, when he surrendered his commission to congress, Col. Tilghman followed the fortunes of his commander and his army. He suffered in the disaster at White Plains; with pain he witnessed the fall of Forts Lee and Washington; he followed in the sad retreat of the apparently dissolving army through the Jerseys into Pennsylvania; he made one of those who, amid storm, darkness and floating ice, embarked in frail boats to cross the Delaware on the famous Christmas night of 1776 with Washington — a deed that has furnished a theme to the poet and a subject to the painter; he claims a part of the glories of Trenton and Princeton; he equally claims a part in the humiliation, without shame, of the defeat at Brandywine, and of the repulse at Germantown; he shared with the army the terrible sufferings at Valley Forge, where indeed he contracted the disease which finally terminated his life; he also bore with that army what is less tolerable than cold and hunger, that long inactivity which resulted from its reduction in numbers that other armies might be filled; he was present aiding and directing that masterly movement by which the army was transferred to the south, to form a junction with its lately arrived allies: and finally, he was

---

[1] Bancroft's *History of the United States*, vol. IX, p. 127.

at Yorktown, actively participating in all the operations of that ever memorable siege and surrender, which was the virtual end of the war.

A few incidents in his military career of a nature almost purely personal, or at least having only an indirect relation to the war, may be noticed. The disastrous battle of Long Island had resulted in the abandonment of New York city by the American forces, and its occupancy by the British. Washington with his army had moved up the Manhattan island and taken post at Haarlem Heights. The convention of the state of New York had become, as it were, a roving body, meeting at various places according to circumstances, and was compelled to adopt unusual means to keep itself informed of the movements of the enemy, domestic and foreign, for, as is known, the lower portion of the state was infested with tories of the most determined and violent character. The convention accordingly appointed a committee of correspondence constituted of these gentlemen: Messrs. William Allison, R. R. Livingston, Henry Wesner and William Duer, for the purpose of obtaining intelligence, and communicating the same to that body. Overtures were made to Col. Tilghman, in a letter of Col. Duer, from Fishkills, of the date of 22nd Sept., 1776, for furnishing a daily letter from head quarters, giving all intelligence that might be received by the commander-in-chief, and all incidents which he thought might be interesting or serviceable to the convention. Col. Tilghman consented to furnish these letters, having the approval of Gen. Washington. An express was provided by the committee for the regular and prompt transmission of the communications. This correspondence continued from September 22nd, to October 21st, 1776. A very considerable number of the letters of the committee to Col. Tilghman and some of his replies are in the hands of his family, and they furnish a most interesting and minute history of the short period which they cover, as well as reveal the feelings of the patriots of the time, both in and out of the army. With reference to the subject of this memoir, they are valuable as indicating his readiness to perform extra official duty to the cause he had espoused, and his ability to perform that duty with credit to himself and acceptance to the committee of the convention. It was of these letters that Gen. Washington is thought to have referred in his letter of condolence to his father, when he said : " If they stand single, as they exhibit a trait of his public character, and like all the rest of his transactions will, I am persuaded, do honor to his understanding and probity, it may be desirable, in this point of view, to keep them alive by mixing them with mine, which, undoubtedly, will claim the attention of the historian." The following taken from his letter of October 3rd, may serve to give an insight into the feelings at head quarters towards those who were serving secretly or openly the royal cause in that part of New York. "I am sorry your convention do not feel themselves legally authorized to make examples of the villains they have apprehended. If that is the case, the well-affected will hardly be able to keep a watch on the ill. The general is determined, if he can, bring some of those in his hands under the denomination of spies, to execute them. General Howe hanged a captain of ours, belonging to Knowlton's Rangers, who went to New York to make discoveries.[1] I do not see why we should not make retaliation." To this Col. Duer replied with equal warmth: "In the name of justice hang two or three of the villains you have apprehended. They will certainly come under the denomination of spies." This correspondence, in which Col. Harrison occasionally took part, in the absence, or preoccupation of Col. Tilghman, on the one hand, and in which Mr. Livingston participated when Mr. Duer was prevented from writing, on the other part, was interrupted by the important movements of the opposing forces, which took place in the autumn of the year, resulting in the transferring of the American army into New Jersey, and later into Pennsylvania. In all these movements, of course, Col. Tilghman was an active agent and participant; but, as has been before stated, as these are matters of familiar history, they need not be noted in this memoir.

The letters of Col. Tilghman which remain rarely make any reference to himself — his wants, his services, his sacrifices or his sufferings. There is admirable reticence about all personal matters. But there is one exception in a letter addressed to the Hon. Robert Morris, and dated Dec. 22, 1780. It would

---

[1] This was *Captain Nathan Hale*, who uttered these heroic words just before his execution: "My only regret is, I have but one life to lay down for my country."

seem that the state of Pennsylvania, from which state he had been appointed to the army, had been negligent in making proper provision for his support — that it had granted him nothing but rations, which he did not need, as with these he was "supplied in the family of his excellency." It seems that his greatest want was personal clothing, for the supply of which his own private means had thus far been used. He says: "I feel a consciousness of speaking the truth when I say that no man has devoted more of his time, and sacrificed more in proportion to his abilities, than I have done in the contest. Whether that time has been well or ill employed I leave it to those who have been acquainted with my services, to determine." His "abilities," that is to say his private fortune, was never large, and the "proportion" of this which he "sacrificed" was very nearly the whole. It is a tradition of his family, but having a more substantial foundation than such orally transmitted accounts of ancestors usually possess, that Col. Tilghman's services for a large part of the time he was in the army were rendered without recompense from congress; for Washington in the letter to Mr. John Sullivan, already quoted, says: "He has been a zealous servant and slave to the public, and a faithful assistant to me for nearly five years, a great part of which time he refused to receive pay." Admirable devotion! with which no meaner motive mingled, not even that of the applause of his countrymen, so freely bestowed upon his great exemplar. In this letter to Mr. Morris, Col. Tilghman, after dismissing his own private affairs, speaks of the embarrassments of the army, and the dangers which were threatening the country; and as this letter has never been published, the following extracts may be a small contribution to the historic literature of the times, which, if it do not reveal anything new, may confirm what is known. Commenting on the policy of enlisting men for short terms of service, which had proved so disastrous, he says: "Instead of securing an army when our money was good, and the people were willing, we have lavished immense sums upon men of an hour, whose terms of service have been spent in marching to and from the army, and in their way devouring like locusts all before them. * * * Two things will save us and that speedily; a sufficient permanent army, and a foreign loan in aid of our resources. We may amuse ourselves with plans of specific requisitions from the states, and a thousand idle projects; but until the army can be paid and fed by the means of a substantial medium, we are only lingering out the time of our dissolution. Can men be expected to serve without provision — without clothing — without pay. Of the last we have had none since March, and no prospect of any. * * * Perhaps there is no man less apt to despond, and I am sure there is none who will oppose longer than I will; but when I see the glorious prize, for which we have been contending, within our reach, if we would but embrace the means of acquiring it, I am sick to death of our folly."

With the year 1781 the war was evidently approaching its conclusion. Washington suddenly withdrawing the army from before New York, which he was threatening, and forming a junction with the French forces under Lafayette on the south, laid siege to Yorktown, Virginia, where Cornwallis was entrenched. Beside his commander was his faithful secretary and aid, Col. Tilghman, who, having gone through the whole contest, was now present at its conclusion. As if prescient that this was to be the decisive and final conflict, immediately upon the American army's taking position, he commenced a daily journal of the siege, which has been preserved to the present, a most interesting memorial of this ever memorable battle, and perhaps, the only one of the kind extant. Time was wanting to him, during the days so filled with stirring events, and active duty, to do more than jot down in fewest words each transaction as it occurred. Elaboration was impossible. Comment out of place. An event, which measured by its results, was one of the most notable in the annals of time, was recorded in this journal with a brevity which is almost sublime. On the 17th October, the British army under Cornwallis virtually, and on the 19th actually and formally, capitulated. Immediately upon the signing of the articles of surrender the commander-in-chief selected one of his staff to be bearer of dispatches to congress, then in session in Philadelphia, that that body might be placed in possession of the joyous intelligence at the earliest moment. Col. Tench Tilghman was selected for this pleasing duty, and he was charged with a letter to the president of congress, Thomas McKean, which, while it announced the great result of the operations before Yorktown, contained these highly complimentary words relating to the bearer: " Sir, * * * Col. Tilghman, one of my aids-de-camp, will have the honor to deliver these dispatches to your excellency. He will be able to inform you of every minute circumstance which is not particularly mentioned in my letter. His merits, which are too well known to need my observations at this time, have gained my particular attention, and I could wish that they may be honored by the notice of your excellency and congress." This intimation of the commander-in-chief that the services of his aid should have some recognition by the supreme powers, was neither forgotten nor neglected, as will be seen in the sequel. The bearer of such intelligence as that with which Col. Tilghman was charged, was not likely to prove a laggard upon his journey. He arrived in Philadelphia on the 23d of the month, having traversed the distance from Yorktown, in about four days, crossing numerous large rivers and probably the Chesapeake bay, between Annapolis and Kent island, for there is no evidence that he passed through Baltimore, which would have been out of his way. As this courier sped along, he spread the happy tidings among an anxious people, who had been long eagerly awaiting intelligence from the scene of operations. He reached his destination in the middle of the night, when the whole city was wrapped in slumber. Impatient to communicate the news, he lost no time in finding the house of the president of congress, whom he aroused, and with him the whole neighborhood, by his vigorous knock at his door. The watchmen of the city taking him to be some roistering young fellow who had bided too long at his cups, were about to arrest him as a disturber of the peace, and confine him in the watch-house till morning. He, however, quickly made known his character and his business, and soon Mr. McKean was in communication with the welcome intruder upon his rest. The news spread with the greatest rapidity through the city, for the watchmen who were ready to arrest him now made the purport of his message the burden of their cry, and as they announced the hour of the night, as was the custom of the day, instead of adhering to the customary formularies respecting the weather, they proclaimed, "Cornwallis is taken." The whole population was soon astir, every one being anxious to have a confirmation of the news by hearing a recital of all the details. Lights appeared at the windows of the houses, so there was a kind of impromptu illumination. The state house bell tolled a joyous peal, like that it sent forth when it proclaimed "liberty throughout the land unto all the inhabitants thereof," in July, '76: and at the dawn of day, which came as the dawn of peace, cannon were fired in honor of the victory, and in exultation over the prospect of independence achieved. Congress met at an earlier hour than usual. The dispatches from Washington were read by the secretary, congratulatory speeches were delivered, and every other expression, comporting with the dignity of such a stately body, was given to the joy which filled every breast.

Of these expressions not the least significant was the going in procession to church, in order to return thanks for the "crowning the allied armies of the United States and France with success." It is not difficult to imagine Col. Tilghman as at once wearied and flattered by the assiduities of the people of Philadelphia — wearied by the frequent repetition of the pleasing story of the surrender, with all the details which the official dispatches omitted, and flattered by the attention and courtesies to which the bearer of such agreeable intelligence was thought to be entitled, and which were so readily and lavishly bestowed. Nor were the compliments and favors confined to the citizens of Philadelphia. A committee of congress, appointed on the 24th of October, and consisting of Messrs. Randolph, Boudinot, Varnum and Carroll, reported on the 29th of that month, a series of resolutions expressive of the thanks of congress to Washington and Lafayette, and to the officers and soldiers under their command; but, in addition, it was ordered that a horse with his caparisons, and a sword, be presented by the board of war to Lieut. Col. Tilghman.[1]

After the battle of Yorktown there were faint gleams which gave promise of the dawn of peace. These continued to increase in brightness until the long wished for orb arose. The army was placed in quarters on the Hudson, and melted gradually away. Respite from labor was given to the officers, many of whom returned to their homes. How Col. Tilghman employed his furloughs, will immediately appear. He

---

[1] For a copy of these resolutions, see apppendix.

still held his connection with the military family, and during his absence from his home in the camp he wrote, not so frequently as was desired, to his friend and commander, receiving in return most kind and affectionate replies. In one of these letters of Gen. Washington to Col. Tilghman, written January 7th, 1783, he uses these words: "I receive with great sensibility your assurances of affection and regard. It would be but a renewal of what I have often repeated to you, that there are few men in the world to whom I am more attached by inclination than I am to you. With the cause, I hope — most devoutly hope — there will soon be an end to my military services — when, as our places of residence will not be far apart, I shall never be more happy than in your company at Mt. Vernon. I shall always be glad to hear from, and keep up a correspondence with you."[1] A man who could win such words from such a man must have had qualities of mind and heart, principles of thought and action, singularly in harmony with those possessed by him who wrote them. If this be a legitimate deduction, can praise go farther than to say, Tilghman was like Washington? But to return. When peace came at last, and the bonds that united the army were to be dissolved, Col. Tilghman participated in that most touching scene, the parting of Washington with his officers, but not with that poignancy of grief that was felt by others, for he was still to accompany him, and stand by his side when, at Annapolis on the 23d of December, 1783, was enacted

---

[1] For this letter see appendix.

that scene, which for moral sublimity is not surpassed in the whole drama of human history, the surrender of his commission as commander-in-chief of the armies of the United States by Gen. Washington. Governed by the same impulses as his great exemplar, Col. Tilghman, from his lower height, stepped down, and he too soon gave up his position and rank, returned with like gladness to the congenial pursuits of peace, and not long after to the wished for joys of wedded life.

During one of the few short furloughs which were accepted by Col. Tilghman whose attention to duty has been likened by Washington to the unceasing toil of the slave, he took occasion to renew his acquaintance with his relatives in the county of his birth, from whom he had so long been separated that they had become as strangers. The soldier who had staked life and fortune upon the result of the struggle for independence would be very naturally attracted to the statesman who had shown equal devotion to the same cause, even if the ties of kinship had not drawn them together. In the year 1779, after visiting his father in Chestertown, whither he had removed from Philadelphia after the commencement of hostilities, Col. Tilghman extended his journey to Talbot, and was welcomed by his uncle, the venerable Matthew Tilghman, at his home upon the Bay-Side.[1] Here

---

[1] This gentleman had occupied positions of trust and distinction under the colonial government, having been for many years one of the county justices, and speaker of the lower house of the general assembly. He took an early and active part in the resistance of the colony to the encroachments of the mother country, and though long unwilling, as most Mary-

he was presented to his cousin, Miss Anna Maria Tilghman, of whose amiable traits, both of person and character, he had already been apprised by his own sisters, who had given him accounts of their agreeable visits to Bay-Side. Naturally susceptible to the influence of female charms, his military service, by withdrawing him in great measure from the society of women, had rendered him more impressible than ever when brought into their presence. It is therefore not wonderful that the soldier, who might be considered yet young in years, and was certainly possessed of the feelings of youth, during this period of respite from duty, of disengagement and almost vacancy of mind, when a kind of dreamy languor had succeeded to the excitement and activity of the camp and field, should have been captivated by the intelligence, amiability and beauty of his cousin. Then, on the other hand, the soft blandishments which the young lady may have really thought were bestowed on the soldier for the sake of the cause which he was championing and defending, or on a relative and guest entitled

---

landers were, to a severance of the political connection which existed between that country and her colony, when the time came for its dissolution, no one was more pronounced in his opinions and decided in his conduct. He was a member of the conventions that were assembled to protest against the arbitrary acts of the royal government; was a delegate to several of the early congresses; was the head of the council of safety of Maryland for the eastern shore; was president of the convention that framed the first constitution of the state of Maryland; and at the date of Col. Tilghman's visit was a member of the senate of the state. From his long and useful public service, from his venerable age, and the universal respect in which he was held, he was called the Patriarch of Maryland. He was a man of large fortune, from which he dispensed a bountiful hospitality, and a liberal charity. He died in 1790.

to them by right of kinship or the laws of hospitality, without any covert design, on her part, completed his capture. The uncertainty of the result of the contest, in which he was then engaged as active participant, prevented him from a formal declaration of his feelings at this time. Three years later, the aspect of public affairs encouraging a hope that the war was not far from an end, and a more intimate acquaintance having confirmed his regard for his cousin, he determined to explain the motives of his conduct and behavior towards the young lady, who, he thought, was entitled to such explanation. But he still was unable to offer her marriage, inasmuch as his fortune was not such as would permit him to maintain her in the style to which she had been accustomed. He, therefore, plainly stated his position, and while expressing his warm affection for her, he said he was unwilling to embarrass her with a formal engagement, but left her free to accept any offers which might be made to her, if the sentiments she felt towards him would permit her so to do. But as common report connected his name with hers, he felt it his duty to apprise her father of what had transpired between them. The letter to the Hon. Matthew Tilghman from Col. Tilghman in reference to this matter, dated June 10th, 1782, is still in existence, in which he asks the privilege of prosecuting his suit, and states that should the father's consent be obtained, he would, ere long, set about the removal of that obstacle to a union with his daughter which was founded in the inadequacy of his income. This letter is admirable for its manliness, its frankness, its delicacy, and its

excellent taste. It is most characteristic of the man.
In it we see united a simple dignity which results from
conscious worth, an unaffected modesty which shrinks
from asserting any special merits, and a self renuncia-
tion which cannot sacrifice the interests of others to
its own gratification. We see too, traces of those
chivalric qualities which had not yet become a mere
survival of a past age, honor towards man and homage
towards woman.[1] To this letter, Mr. Tilghman gave
a favorable reply. Now it was that Col. Tilghman
found the prudence of which he thought himself possessed was not proof against the impatience which
prompted him to have the marriage concluded. He
who was so cautious that he was unwilling to enter
into any formal engagement until the war was over,
and he had secured such an income as would support
a wife in a manner becoming her station, was now
ready and anxious, though peace had not been declared, and though he had embarked in no business,
that an early day should be appointed for the fruition
of his hopes and desires. It was determined that the
marriage should be solemnized in the winter of 1782,[2]

---

[1] For this letter see appendix.

[2] The head quarters of the army, after the capitulation at Yorktown, had been established at Newburgh, on the Hudson. Many of the troops had been permitted to return home, and leaves of absence granted to some of the officers. Col. Tilghman availed himself of the opportunity to visit Talbot, and his time passed so pleasantly there that he had been some- what negligent of his correspondence with his friend and chief. His long absence and infrequent letters appeared to give plausibility to a rumor which had reached head-quarters that he was married; and a letter written to his commander in June or July, 1782, in which he referred to his expected change of condition, with a vagueness of expression, for which his modesty will sufficiently account, seemed to confirm the report. Gen.

but the illness of Mr. Charles Carroll, the barrister, who had married an elder sister, which illness indeed finally terminated his life, caused the postponement of the nuptials until June 9, 1783, when they were duly celebrated, with much quietness and privacy, on account of the recent family affliction just mentioned. He received, among those of other friends, the congratulations of General and Mrs. Washington, in a letter couched in the following kind and affectionate language: " Why have you been so niggardly in communicating your change of condition to us, or to the world? By dint of enquiries we have heard of your marriage; but have scarcely got a confirmation of it yet. On the presumption however that it is so, I offer you my warmest congratulations and best wishes for the enjoyment of many happy years; in both of which Mrs. Washington joins me very cordially."[1] The lady with whom Col. Tilghman was thus happily united was possessed of many of those graces which win and those qualities which retain the admiration and respect of men. Her manners were most gracious, condescending to those below her in the social scale and engaging to her equals. Without pretensions to high culture, either in the lighter accomplishments, or the more solid acquirements, for which her residence in the country afforded small opportunity, she was nevertheless intelligent, as well as naturally endowed with a most excellent judgment. The habit

---

Washington's pleasant and almost playful reply to this letter, may be found in the appendix, and affords another proof of the affectionate regard which he felt for Col. Tilghman.

[1] For this letter see appendix.

of her father of conversing with her freely and constantly upon public business, and his custom of having her with him at Annapolis when attending to colonial or state affairs, and at Philadelphia when serving in congress, made her familiar with the political movements and stirring events of the time. When thrown upon her own resources after his and her husband's death, she manifested most excellent capacity for the conduct of her private affairs. Nor was she devoid of literary skill, as is shown by an inedited memoir of her father, which she left behind her, and her numerous letters. In religion she was of the church of England, and its successor in America; and while holding to its doctrines with the tenacity of conviction, she was most liberal and tolerant of the opinions of those who differed from her in belief. Living at the time when the conflict for supremacy in her county was raging between the old church and Methodism, its child, she was able to retain the love and respect of those whom she opposed. Without affecting the spirituality, which to her seemed so like sanctimoniousness, and which was the religious fashion of the day, she was in sentiment and conduct deeply pious. To her servants or slaves she was mild and indulgent; to her neighbors kind and obliging; to her friends and relatives most affectionate. Her house was the very home of hospitality. Her wealth was the store from which charity drew her most bountiful supplies for the surrounding poor. She lived to a great age, retaining her faculties to the end unimpaired, honored and revered by all, beloved by her children and her children's children to the third generation. She cherished to the last memories of her early lost husband. It was a duty, held as almost sacred, annually, upon the recurrence of the anniversary of her marriage, to retire to a private room, and taking from their repository all the relics of her deceased husband, which she preserved with the most scrupulous care, for a while to indulge herself in the tender and mournful reminiscences suggested by these mementos, and then to lay them away again in their proper receptacle, made sweet and safe with fragrant herbs and aromatic gums. Of this lady Gen. Lafayette retained kindly memories, and when he was in this country in 1824, in a letter written in reply to one of a committee of the citizens of Queen Anne's, congratulating him upon his arrival in America, presenting their homage for his services and merit, and inviting him to their county, he said : "It is my eager and affectionate wish to visit the Eastern Shore of this state. I anticipate the pleasure there to recognize several of my companions in arms, and among the relations of my departed friends, to find the honored widow of a dear brother in General Washington's family, Col. Tilghman, as well as a daughter of my friend Carmichæl,[1] who first received the secret vows of my engagement in the American cause, the least suspicion of which by the French or British government it was at that time momentous for me to prevent." For many years preceding her death, she had been the recipient from the government

---

[1] Mr. Carmichæl was secretary to the American commissioners, at Paris, and a resident of Queen Anne's county, Maryland.

of a pension, in consideration of the meritorious services of Col. Tilghman : but no discharge was ever made of the claims which he justly had against that government for arrearages of pay, but which, it is due to his memory to say, were never demanded.

As soon as a prospect of peace was disclosed, and before the war was actually ended, Col. Tilghman began his preparations for a return to his original occupation of merchant, when the army should be disbanded, and he relieved from his military duties. Upon the signing of the articles by which national independence was acknowledged, he was urged by General Washington to continue in the military service of the United States. Before the resignation of the commander-in-chief he had recommended to congress that it should not rely for defence against foreign aggression, or domestic commotion upon the uncertain militia levies of the states, but should provide for a small body of well trained professional soldiers. Although congress had shown great reluctance to adopt this advice, sharing as it did the popular apprehension, founded upon past experience, that a standing army is more frequently an instrument of oppression than a means of defence; yet, the commander-in-chief foresaw that political exigencies would soon require that body to follow his suggestions. Hence his advice to Col. Tilghman to maintain his military connection. This gentleman, however, if ever he had been inclined to follow the advice of his commander, which is doubtful, for the pursuits of peace were more in accordance with his natural disposition and his early training, when he saw the indisposition of congress to retain or organize a force commensurate with the national dignity, declined remaining in a service which was calculated to bring ridicule rather than honor from the insignificance of the command, and in which the emoluments were likely to be both small and uncertain. His private means had been sadly impaired by the war, now happily closed. His small fortune, realized before the war, which was constituted of the personal obligations of those who had become indebted to him in his short mercantile adventures, was almost swept away by the bankruptcy of some, and by the payment by others of their indebtedness in a depreciated currency, as he mentions in his private letters still extant.[1] In common with most of his countrymen of that day he indulged the opinion that the country was about to enter upon a grand career of industrial prosperity; and that as soon as the domestic ports should be opened to the trade of the world, and the foreign to the shipping of the new nation, commerce would not only fill its old channels, but open new, to pour a flood of wealth upon the people of America. It was a period of great hopefulness, although many who had been speculating upon the continuance of the war, were ruined by the coming of peace.

The city of Baltimore was just entering upon that career of prosperity, which at that day was unprecedented in this country, and which has hardly been surpassed by any more recent examples of progress.

---

[1] See appendix.

The spreading of the settlements towards the west, to which she was in nearer proximity than any of the other seaboard towns, gave promise that Baltimore was to become a great emporium, a promise which is yet in process of realization. Col Tilghman resolved to settle at this favorable point, hoping to share in the prosperity which was so evidently waiting to reward the commercial enterprise of her citizens. At first he engaged in trade upon his own account, but soon finding the field so favorable as well as so wide, inviting and demanding larger capital, more extended connections and greater credit than he could command, he was glad to accept overtures to a partnership with a gentleman well known in commercial circles both in Europe and America, of large experience in business, of ample means and of abilities of the first order, as had been shown by his management of the finances of the country during the war of the revolution. These overtures were made by Mr. Robert Morris, who, at that time, occupied the most conspicuous position in commerce of any man of his day in America. He had known Col. Tilghman from his youth, and had learned, before the war, to appreciate his capacity and integrity. His merits were further discovered during the contest, when Mr. Morris was thrown into frequent intercourse with him. Among the interesting documents still preserved by the descendants of Col. Tilghman is that containing the articles of copartnership between him and Mr. Morris. These articles bear the date of January 1st, 1784, and were to be in force for the term of seven years. By them, the parties agreed to enter into a mercantile business, of the precise nature of which it is not easy to determine, but apparently, it was a shipping and commission business, in which, while the produce and merchandise of others were sold for a percentage, the partners made foreign adventures upon their own account. Mr. Morris continued to reside in Philadelphia, while Mr. Tilghman conducted the business in Baltimore. It does not appear that Col. Tilghman had any interest in the Philadelphia house of his partner. The style of the firm in Baltimore was, Tench Tilghman and Company. The amounts invested by the partners were, "£5000 current money of Maryland, in specie, at the rate of seven shillings to the Mexican dollar." and £2500 of the same kind of money, for Mr. Morris and Col. Tilghman respectively; and they were to divide the profits equally, but Col. Tilghman was entitled to £400 annually, over and above his proportionable part "in consideration of his residence in Baltimore." The signature of Mr. Morris was witnessed by his Philadelphia partner Mr. Swanwick and Governeur Morris. That of Col. Tilghman by John Richardson and Jacob Sampson. The copartnership thus begun continued to the early death of the junior of the firm in 1786, an event the sadness of which had this late alleviation, that he was spared the humiliation and loss which would have come through the subsequent bankruptcy of Mr. Morris, and was saved from the patriot's mortification of seeing the man, whose financial wisdom and self-sacrificing devotion had sustained his country's armies in the darkest hours, occupy a debtor's prison.[1]

The business career of Col. Tilghman illustrated those two qualities of heart and mind which characterize as well as dignify the true merchant: perfect integrity in all that relates to others, and soundness of judgment in all that relates to himself — qualities that permit the doing no wrong and the suffering none — the very qualities that marked the true knight

---

[1] There was another tie which connected Mr. Morris and Col. Tilghman: the fathers of each had been acquainted in Talbot county, Maryland, and there the latter had received his early education. The first Robert Morris was a merchant at Oxford, Md., acting as agent or factor of Foster Cunliffe & Co. of Liverpool. He was killed by a wad from a cannon fired as a salute to im, and lies buried at old White Marsh church, about six miles from Oxford, where there is a tomb stone with this inscription :

> In Memory
> of
> Robert Morris, a native of Liverpool
> In Great Britain.
> Late a Merchant of Oxford,
> In this Province.
> Punctual integrity influenced his dealings;
> Principles of Honor governed his actions;
> With an uncommon degree of sincerity,
> He despised artifice and dissimulation.
> His Friendship was fair candid and valuable;
> His Charity, frequent, secret and well adapted;
> His zeal for the public good active and useful;
> His Hospitality was enhanced by his conversation,
> Seasoned with cheerful wit and sound judgment.
> A salute from the cannon of a ship,
> (The wad fracturing his arm)
> Was the signal by which he departed,
> Greatly lamented, as he was esteemed,
> In the fortieth year of his age,
> On the 12th day of July,
> 1750.

in a chivalrous age. That he possessed these qualities is attested by the words and acts of two most eminent men, who were not only themselves endowed with them, but who had had every opportunity of discovering their existence in him — Mr. Robt. Morris and Gen. Washington. Mr. Morris had known him in business before the war; he had known him as the trusted secretary of the commander-in-chief during that whole contest; and this long acquaintance had inspired him with such confidence in his good-sense and honesty as to prompt him to the most intimate connection in trade. But after the copartnership had been formed, Mr. Morris, as his letters, still extant, show, took pains to give repeated assurance to his partner of his implicit reliance upon his honor and his abilities as a merchant. These assurances are couched in the most delicate and flattering terms, and lay in a touch of color amidst the neutral tints of a business correspondence. Gen. Washington, by his long association with Col. Tilghman, had acquired a similar confidence in his entire probity and good sense; for upon his retirement to Mount Vernon, his old secretary and aid became his factor or agent in Baltimore for the transaction of almost every kind of business. Col. Tilghman sold the products of his estates, as far as they were disposed of in that city: he was the purchaser of all articles for domestic and plantation use, even to the china that adorned Mrs. Washington's tea-table, or to her own and the general's personal clothing. He made contracts with workmen for building; he hired servants from the emigrant ships; he selected and stipulated with the gentleman who was to act as private tutor to Mrs. Washington's children and as secretary to the general; in short, there was nothing which the general required should be done, important or trifling, that was not performed by his old confidential secretary but now equally trusted friend and commercial agent. The most unreserved confidence seems to have been reposed in him; and what he did was always approved. If better and additional evidence were wanting of Gen. Washington's confidence in Col. Tilghman as the capable and upright merchant, it would be afforded by a letter still extant, in which a request by the former is made of the latter, that he would receive into his counting room a young person, a relative, to acquire a knowledge of business. From what is known of Gen. Washington's prudence and discretion, this act of his, though in the form of a favor asked, must be regarded as a compliment bestowed; for it is not probable that he would have sought to place a youth, with whom he was personally connected, under the care and training of a man who had not shown himself possessed of those qualities which he would wish to be cultivated in one in whose welfare he felt an interest.[1]

Although Col. Tilghman was immersed in business he found time to think and write of politics, municipal, state and national. His writing, at a time when newspapers were not so common as now, was confined to private correspondence. He maintained, to within a few weeks of his death, frequent intercourse by letters,

---
[1] See appendix.

with his father-in-law Mr. Matthew Tilghman, who had long taken an active part in politics, as has been before mentioned. This correspondence, of which there are some remains, was an interesting *mélange* of family, business and public affairs. It would seem that he, like most thoughtful men of the time, entertained grave apprehensions of the success of the new government under the articles of confederation. The weaknesses of this government betrayed themselves during the progress of the war; but the enthusiasm of patriotism compensated in large measure for its lack of inherent vigor, and carried on the contest, in some halting and hesitating, but, in the end, successful way to a fortunate conclusion. After the war was over, and the power of a government had to take the place of zeal for a cause, its feebleness became more and more apparent, and disorganization or subjection to some strong hand seemed inevitable. The following extract from a letter of Col. Tilghman to the Hon. Matthew Tilghman, bearing the date of February 5th, 1786, expresses the apprehensions that were entertained of the stability of the government of the United States, for some years after the acknowledgment of their independence: "It is a melancholy truth, but so it is, that we are at this time the most contemptible and abject nation on the face of the earth. We have neither reputation abroad nor union at home. We hang together merely because it is not the interest of any other power to shake us to pieces, and not from any well cemented bond of our own. How should it be otherwise? The best men we have are all basking at home in lucrative posts, and we send the scum to represent us in the grand national council. France has met us there on equal terms. Instead of keeping a man of rank as minister at our court, she sends a person in quality of *chargé des affaires*, who was but a degree above a domestic in the family of the late minister. All joking apart, I view our federal affairs as in the most desperate state. I have long been convinced that we cannot exist as republics. We have too great a contrariety of interests ever to draw together. It will be a long time before any one man will be hardy enough to undertake the task of uniting us under one head. I do not wish to see the time. One revolution has been sufficient for me, but sure I am another of some kind will take place much earlier than those who do not think deeply on the subject suppose." From this letter it is very evident that Col. Tilghman had clearly recognized the failure of the confederation of states, and that he had no hope that any modification of the articles of this league of separate republics, by which the independence of each was to be maintained, would perpetuate a government so loosely hung together, and with so little autonomic power to secure obedience to its requirements. It is also clear that he had not relieved his mind of the illusion fostered and perpetuated by monarchy, that by the mind and hand of a single person only could union and harmony be secured. He had not yet learned to trust to the wisdom of the people, so like a political instinct, to effect what he thought was beyond the power of such

statesmanship as was embodied in our legislatures.
It is evident he was anticipating another revolution,
in which some strong hand should harness the recalcitrant states, and seizing the reins of power, direct
the car of the united nation upon the road of progress.
The revolution, which with an admirable prescience
he had anticipated, came soon after the words above
quoted were written, but it came in a manner which
his political astrology had not enabled him to foresee.
The formation of the constitution of 1787 was the
work of the people, who had discovered the necessity
of a "more perfect union." The evils which were expected, by Col. Tilghman and those who thought like
him, to flow from any attempt at the unification of
the heterogeneous elements of the confederacy, were
happily not realized; at least not realized until many
years later, when the sentiment of nationality, once
a germ immature and weak, had so rooted itself to
the soil, and so spread itself in the air of the popular
mind, that it was able to withstand the storm of civil
war. One other reflection, suggested by this letter
may be pardoned. The complaint that he utters of
the insufficiency of those who were sent to the
"national council" is one, as appears, that has been
made at every period in our history. We are therefore encouraged to believe that the public men of the
present day, however much they may fall below our
ideals of true statesmen, are not worse than those who
preceded them, whose actions, we think, were
prompted by an unselfish sentiment, and regulated by
a far-reaching wisdom, and whose memories we now

revere as those of the very fathers of the republic. In view of the great prosperity we have enjoyed, under legislation conducted by men whom Col. Tilghman has designated as "the scum," we may indulge the hope that those who we think are to be characterized as both ignorant and dishonest, may not bring utter ruin upon the country? Some how, and yet we know not why, from the conflicts of ignorance, wherever thought is free, the light of truth is elicited, and from the decomposition of corruption, wherever political action is unrestrained by arbitrary power, the germ of right is developed.

Belonging to a family of the Maryland gentry of the highest respectability and social prominence; connected by kinship or friendship with the very best people of the province or state; endowed with those fine sensibilities which would have made him the gentleman, had he not been such by birth; possessed of a vigorous mind trained in the best schools of the country, and in those better schools, an intercourse with great men, and a participation in great affairs; adorned with manners which were at once the expression of an inherited courtesy, and the reflection of the polite circles in which he had moved; it would have been strange if the house of Col. Tilghman had not become the resort of all the cultivated, refined and distinguished of the commonwealth.[1] There could be seen occasionally many who had national repute and whose names have now a historic im-

---

[1] The house of Col. Tilghman was situated upon Lombard street, near Howard, opposite the meeting house of the Friends.

portance. There he dispensed a generous, but not ostentatious, hospitality to all whom he enrolled among his friends, and particularly to his old companions in arms. There he entertained Lafayette during his first visit to America after the revolution, in 1784.[1] There too he had the satisfaction, according to traditions in the family, of occasionally welcoming his old commander, Gen. Washington, when he visited Baltimore — joyful days, to be marked by a whiter stone.

While thus treading the difficult path of a busy career, yet always

"Wearing the white flower of a blameless life;"

while enjoying the comforts and delights of a happy home which refinement graced and which affection ruled; while surrounded by kind and appreciating friends, followed by the honoring respect of his fellow citizens, and distinguished above most others by the high regard and warm attachment of the most notable man of his day; while wealth accumulated and flattered him with the prospect of affluence and elegant ease; the one bitter drop in the cup of life that flavored every draught, was the presence of that malady which he had contracted through hardship and exposure endured while in the army, and which without pause had been making inroads upon his constitution. The warnings he received by his occasional illnesses, when the nature of the disease gave small hope of

---

[1] The bedstead upon which this friend of America slept while visiting Col. Tilghman in Baltimore, was sacredly preserved by Mrs. Tilghman during her long life, and is still kept as an interesting relic by her descendants.

complete restoration, were of little more service than to exhort one, who needed no such exhortation, to temperateness and regularity of living. Early in the year 1786 his disease was evidently approaching a crisis, which he was encouraged by his friends and physicians to expect would be favorable. In a letter written to his father-in-law in February of that year, after the more painful symptoms of a severe attack of hepatic abscess had abated, he expressed a hope, that having passed with safety the most critical period, he would soon be able to enjoy his usual health, a hope which he seems to have shared with his medical advisers. But soon there was a return of the same distressing symptoms, of which there was no alleviation; but a gradual increase in severity until the 18th of April, when he was relieved of his sufferings by the kindly hand of death, at the early age of forty-one years. His illness was assuaged, as far as this was possible, by all the attention and care which the most affectionate solicitude could bestow, and the bitterness of death itself by the consolations of religion, for he held to the faith of his fathers, which was that of the church of England. His body was interred in the old burial ground of Saint Paul's, in the city of Baltimore, whence it was removed to the cemetery on Lombard stret, where his remains still lie.[1]

"Multis ille bonis flebilis occidit."

---

[1] The following inscription may be found upon a plain slab over his grave in the burial ground, no longer used for the interment of the dead, situated on Lombard street between Green and Paca streets, in the city of Baltimore:

He died lamented by all good men. At his funeral his fellow citizens and brethren in arms gave every suitable token of their appreciation of his worth, and of their affectionate regard. The public journals, both of the city of Baltimore and of Philadelphia, at a

---

In Memory of
Col. Tench Tilghman,
Who died April 18th, 1786,
In the 42nd year of his age,
Very much lamented.
He took an early and active part
In the great contest that secured
The Independence of
The United States of America.
He was an Aid-de-Camp to
His Excellency General Washington
Commander in chief of the American armies,
And was honored
With his friendship and confidence,
And
He was one of those
Whose merits were distinguished
And
Honorably rewarded
By the Congress
But
Still more to his Praise
He was
A good man.

After the death of the widow of Col. Tilghman, their daughter, Mrs. Nicholas Goldsborough, and grandson, General Tench Tilghman, erected a handsome monument to her, which became also a cenotaph to him, at Plimhimmon near Oxford, Talbot county, Maryland. This monument, consisting of a pedestal and obelisk, has inscribed upon it the following epitaphs:

To Mrs. Anna Maria Tilghman.

The affection and Veneration of a daughter and grandson have caused them to erect this Monument to Anna Maria Tilghman, daughter of the Hon. Matthew Tilghman and widow of Lt. Col. Tilghman. Her pure character, combining every christian grace and virtue, attracted the

Memoir of Lt. Col. Tench Tilghman. 63

time when it was not so common as now to praise the dead almost without discrimination, published obituary notices which were expressive of the general sorrow for his early demise, and of the high esteem in which he was held wherever his character was known.[1] Nor were these public testimonials the only

devoted love of her family connections, and the admiration and esteem of all who knew her.

Born July 17th, 1755.
Died Jan. 13th, 1843.

Tench Tilghman, Lt. Col. in the Continental army and Aid-de-camp of Washington, who spoke of him thus: He was in every action in which the main army was concerned. A great part of the time he refused to receive pay. While living no man could be more esteemed, and since dead none more lamented. No one had imbibed sentiments of greater friendship for him than I had done. He left as fair a reputation as ever belonged to a human character.

Died April 18th, 1786.
Aged 42 years.

[1] The following is from a paper of Philadelphia, being part of a notice of his death: "Lately departed this life at Baltimore in the State of Maryland, Tench Tilghman, Esq.; a gentleman no less distinguished for public than for private virtues. Of the former, it is enough to say, that during the late war he was the confidential secretary and aid-de-camp of the illustrious commander-in-chief of the American forces. Of the latter, his punctuality, integrity and regularity as a merchant — his excellent deportment as a citizen, parent and friend, and general benevolence as a man, will long remain the precious testimonials. He bore the rank of lieut. colonel in the army from 1777, to its being disbanded. He received the last public acknowledgment from his great chief on the 19th of October, 1781, on the occasion of the surrender of Lord Cornwallis and his army — an event which he was sent to notify to congress, who thereupon, on the 29th of the same month voted him their plaudit of his merit and abilities."

The following is from *Maryland Journal and Baltimore Advertiser* of Friday, April 21, 1786:

"Yesterday evening were interred, in St. Paul's church yard, with the greatest marks of respect, the remains of the late Col. Tench Tilghman, an eminent merchant of this town. He departed this life on Tuesday evening, after languishing a long time under a most distressing illness, in tributes to his worth. Private letters from persons of the first distinction, attest his merit, and furnish his best eulogium. Mr. Sparks in his *Life and Writings of Washington* says: "Several of Gen. Washington's correspondents spoke of his death with much warmth of feeling." Robert Morris said: " You have

the 42d year of his age. In public life his name stands high as a *soldier* and patriot, his political conduct during the late war having entitled him to the noblest praise, that of an *independent honest man* — and his services in the honorable and confidential character of aid-de-camp to his Excellency General Washington, in the course of the late glorious contest for *Freedom* and *Independence*, deservedly obtained the approbation of his chief and his country. As a private character, the deep affection of his family, the sorrow of his friends, and the universal regret of his fellow citizens, best show their sense of the heavy loss they have sustained, in the death of this worthy and amiable man."

The following tribute to Col. Tilghman, was published in the *Portfolio*, and was from the pen of Mr. Swanwick, the business partner in Philadelphia of Mr. Robert Morris. This gentleman's long and intimate acquaintance with Col. Tilghman and his own high character give to his elegiac verses a value which they do not derive from their poetical merit.

To the Memory of the late
TENCH TILGHMAN, ESQ., OF BALTIMORE.

Ye Muses! weep o'er Tilghman's sacred tomb,
And plant around it flowers of endless bloom:
Oh! be it yours to eternize his name,
And sound your lyres to his immortal fame.
And then Oh Honor, parent of the brave,
Keep constant vigil at thy soldier's grave;
Let no rude step profane the awful shade,
Where pious hands have now his ashes laid.
Thou too Columbia, mistress of the soil,
To whom devoted was his martial toil,
Place high his ensigns, in that pile august
Which thou shalt raise, hereafter from the dust-
To hold the archives of thy splendid reign,
And all thy warlike trophies to contain.
Oh! think how faithful, in each trying hour,
Thy Tilghman fought to elevate that power;
And let a tear drop grateful on his urn

lost in him a most faithful and valuable friend. He was to me the same. I esteemed him very much and I lament his loss exceedingly." Gen. Knox in a letter to his widow, hereafter quoted in full, says: "Death has deprived you of a most tender and virtuous companion, and the United States of an able and upright patriot. When time shall have smoothed

>Which honor guards, and all the Muses mourn.
>Death! How sure the arrows sped by thee!
>Could worth have stayed them, Tilghman had been free.
>But no! thy altars glory in the tide
>Of precious blood, by fall of chiefs supplied.
>Who next shall yield to thy relentless stroke,
>Which while it tears the ivy rends the oak.
>What nobler victim can thy grasp attain,
>Till his great master falls amidst the slain?
>Oh Washington! thy aid has gone before
>To sound thy glories on that deathless shore,
>Where rest the great, the good of every age,
>Who deck the poet's or the historian's page.
>The crowd illustrious now await thy flight,
>From shades terrestrial to eternal light:
>Where to the laurels, thine so justly due,
>They'll add a wreath immortal to thy brow.
>This scene triumphant 'tis thy aid prepares,
>And thus he sooths his absence from thy cares.
> What various honors, Tilghman, knew thy days!
>The warrrior's trophy bound with civic lays!
>Whether as merchant, patriot or friend,
>Husband or parent, we alike commend:
>In every walk found equally to shine,
>Thine were the social, all the virtues thine.
>A friend inscribes this column to thy praise,
>With mournful heart, but with imperfect lays.
>Enough for him, if true to merit's claim,
>These lines attest how spotless was thy fame,
>And call some bard, more skilled, in future verse
>Thy splendid deeds more nobly to rehearse,
>In times when poets shall arise to crown,
>America's great worthies with renown.

the severities of your grief, you will derive consolation from the reflection that Colonel Tilghman acted well his part in the theatre of human life, and that the supreme authority of the United States have expressly given their sanction to his merit." But, considering their source, as well as their character, the highest testimonials were those which proceeded from Gen. Washington himself. To be praised by this great man is fame. In a letter to Thomas Jefferson dated August 1st, 1786, he says: "You will probably have heard of the death of Gen. Greene before this reaches you; in which case you will in common with your countrymen have regretted the loss of so great, and so honest a man. Gen. McDougall, who was a brave soldier and a disinterested patriot, is also dead. He belonged to the legislature of his state. The last act of his life was (after being carried on purpose to the senate), to give his voice against the emission of a paper currency. Col. Tilghman, who was formerly of my family, died lately, and left as fair a reputation as ever belonged to a human character. Thus some of the pillars of the revolution fall. May our country never want props to support the glorious fabric." Again: in a letter of condolence addressed to Mr. James Tilghman, the father of Col. Tilghman, dated June 5th, 1786, at Mount Vernon, a letter the original of which is sacredly preserved by the family, and from which this extract is made, Gen. Washington uses these words: "Of all the numerous acquaintances of your lately deceased son, and amidst all the sorrowings that are mingled on that melancholy occasion, I may venture to assert (that excepting those of his nearest relatives) none could have felt his death with more regret than I did, because no one entertained a higher opinion of his worth or had imbibed sentiments of greater friendship for him than I had done. That you, sir, should have felt the keenest anguish for this loss, I can readily conceive — the ties of parental affection, united with those of friendship could not fail to have produced this effect. It is however a dispensation, the wisdom of which is inscrutable; and amidst all your grief, there is this consolation to be drawn; that while living no man could be more esteemed, and since dead, none more lamented than Col. Tilghman."[1] One so praised, and by such a man, is surer of an immortality of fame, than those for whom a Roman senate once decreed a triumph.

The order of congress, to which reference has already been made, passed upon the occasion of the surrender at Yorktown, of which happy event Col. Tilghman was deputed the messenger to bear the intelligence to that body, that there should be presented to this officer a horse and a sword, as a token of the gratification experienced upon the reception of the news and also as a recognition of the merit and services of the herald himself, to which the letter of the commander-in-chief to the president had so pointedly called attention, and so explicitly asked some public testimonial, was not carried fully into effect until after the death

---

[1] This letter of Gen. Washington, which will be found printed entire in the appendix to this memoir, furnishes the vindication of that commander from the charges which were made by Capt. Asgil, after his release and return to England.

of him whom it meant to honor. He had the gratification, however, before his demise, to receive from Gen. Knox, secretary of war, a letter dated Dec. 7th, 1785, in which was inclosed an order on the treasury for four hundred dollars, to purchase the horse and accoutrements. This letter concluded thus: "I expect in a month or two to receive all the swords which were voted by congress as testimonies of their special approbation. Upon receiving them I shall have the pleasure of transmitting yours." Unfortunately the declining health of Col. Tilghman deprived him of the gratification of mounting the horse, and his death soon after, of the pleasure of wearing or even receiving the sword, voted by his country. Soon after his decease, however, Mrs. Tilghman was the recipient of a letter from Gen. Knox as flattering to the memory of her late husband as it was gratifying to herself, of which the following is a copy:

War Office of the United States,
New York, May 30, 1786.

MADAM:

I have the honor to enclose for your satisfaction, a copy of a resolve of congress of the 29th October, 1781.

During the last year I had the honor of presenting to Col. Tilghman the horse, agreeably to the direction of the resolve, and I then mentioned to him that I should forward the sword as soon as it should be finished.

But death, the inevitable tribute of our system, has permanently deprived you of the most tender and virtuous companion, and the United States of an able and upright patriot. While you are overwhelmed with affliction, your friends unavailingly condole with you on an event, which they could not prevent, and to which they also must submit.

When time shall have smoothed the severities of your grief, you will derive consolation from the reflection that Col. Tilghman acted well his part on the theatre of human life; and that the supreme authority of the United States, have expressly given their sanction to his merit.

The sword directed to be presented to him, which I have the honor to transmit to you, will be an honorable and perpetual evidence of his merit and of the applause of his country.

    I have the honor to be, Madam,
        with perfect respect,
your most obedient and very humble servant,
                H. KNOX.

The sword thus gracefully presented to the widow of Col. Tilghman, and so sadly received by her, was piously preserved with many other relics associated with his military career; and now, having passed through the hands of two generations of his descendants, it remains in the possession of his great grandson Oswald Tilghman, Esq., of Easton, Maryland.[1]

Upon the institution of the society of the Cincinnati in 1783, for the purpose of perpetuating " as well the rembembrance of the late bloody conflict

---

[1] This sword was made in Paris. It is the usual officers' dress sword with rapier blade and gold and silver mountings. Upon the handle is engraved the insignia of the Society of the Cincinnati, and these words: " Presented to Lieut. Col. Tench Tilghman by Congress, Oct. 19, 1781."

of eight years, as the mutual friendships which were formed under the pressure of common danger," Col. Tilghman became a member, and received as a present from the president general, his excellency, Geo. Washington, the order or decoration of this society, which yet remains in the hands of his descendant, Mr. Oswald Tilghman, in the same condition as it was presented. A grand-son, Gen. Tench Tilghman, was president of the society for Maryland, at the time of his death in 1874, and had been appointed its historiographer.

Col. Tilghman left two children, daughters, one of whom was a posthumous child. The eldest of these married Mr. Tench Tilghman, son of Peregrine Tilghman, of Hope, from whom has sprung a numerous family. The youngest married Col. Nicholas Goldsborough, of Ottwell, from whom also has come many descendants. All of these have a just pride in an ancestor whose life illustrated some of the best virtues of human character, and many have exhibited traits not unworthy of their distinguished lineage. After the death of her husband Mrs. Tilghman returned to her father's house on Bay-side, of Talbot county, but subsequently removed to her beautiful estate of Plimhimmon, near Oxford, in the same county, which Mr. Matthew Tilghman had purchased for his daughter. Here she lived in great comfort and simple elegance to the advanced age of eighty-eight years, surrounded by her children and her children's children, and loved and venerated by all who were privileged to come within the circle of her acquaintance or scope

Memoir of Lt. Col. Tench Tilghman. 71

of her charities. Pious affection has dedicated a handsome monument to her memory and that of her husband, as has before been mentioned.[1]

Of Col. Tilghman there are several portraits, one, a miniature, by an unknown artist, taken from life, and represented to be a very exact likeness, is in the hands of a grand-daughter, Mrs. Margaretta (Goldsborough) Hollyday. From this has been taken, by heliotype process, the portrait that accompanies this memoir. In the painting, more meritorious than well known, of the capitulation at Yorktown, by Charles Wilson Peale, now in the house of delegates of the state of Maryland at Annapolis, Col. Tilghman is represented in a life size figure standing beside Gen. Washington, holding in his hands a scroll, inscribed " Articles of Capitulation, York, Gloster, and dependencies, April 19, 1781." As this picture was executed soon after the event it commemorates, it is believed the portraits were taken from life, or from studies from life. That of Washington is regarded as especially accurate, both as to features and bearing. As Mr. Peale was an acquaintance and friend of Col. Tilghman, it is thought the portrait of him, one of the principal figures in the painting, is equally accurate. Lafayette stands beside him. In the Athenæum at Hartford, Connecticut, there is a painting by Col. John Trumbull, representing a scene in the battle of Trenton. It is thought by some critics to be the most impressive of the works of this artist in that celebrated collection. The central group is

---

[1] For the inscription upon this monument see page 62.

composed of Gen. Washington, Col. Tilghman, Col. Harrison, Col. Smith, and the wounded Hessian officer Col. Rahl. The three first mentioned are mounted. The representation of Col. Tilghman in this painting also, is thought to be a true portrait. There is a fourth portrait in the city of Trenton, in a painting, a particular description of which has not been obtained.

The personal appearance of Col. Tilghman was that of a gentleman of medium height and slender form. His complexion was fresh and florid, his eyes gray, and his hair a rich auburn, worn in queue, according to the fashion of the day. He was not insensible to the advantages of dress, in which he was scrupulously neat and regardful of the mode. His modesty gave to his bearing the reserve of hauteur, and though repelling familiarity, he was never wanting in courtesy, while to friends his manners were most cordial.

In this memoir the extravagance of praise, to which the biographer is prone, has been shunned as not befitting the ingenuous character of him whose memory it is designed to refresh and perpetuate. If the merits of Col. Tilghman had been fewer in number and lower in order than they really were, there still would be no need to exaggerate them in order to commend him to the esteem and admiration of good men. Even the eulogist seeking how best to praise him, finds "the simple truth his highest skill"—finds that he cannot better speak of him than by a frank relation of his life; and that any words spoken of him, not marked by the same fairness and candor that belonged to him of whom they should be uttered, would be rebuked by recollections of his pure and upright character. It is not pretended that he belonged to that small class of men, the very great

"Lights of the world and demigods of fame:"

men who by their deeds have changed the fortunes of nations; who have enlightened the world by their discoveries in science, benefited it by their inventions of usefulness, or delighted it with their creations in art or literature. As a soldier he was no leader of great armies to victory or destruction; as a citizen he was no projector of novel policies of government to bless or blight his country; as a man of affairs he was no pioneer of a new commerce, no founder of a new industry, to bring riches or ruin upon the land. He was none of these. He was the patriot soldier with whose motives mingled no desire of personal aggrandizement nor ignoble ambition, as his long and unpaid service of his country, and "that sublime repression of himself" in surrendering precedence of promotion to others, for the good of the cause, attest. He was the honorable merchant, who in his dealings knew not how to deviate from the line of rectitude; whom no suggestions of political passion could tempt to wrong even the enemies of his country; whom no opportunities, afforded by unjust laws, invited to an evasion of his obligations. To his perfect probity let his provision, when the war broke out, for the full payment of his English creditors, and his refusal to avail himself of the legal authorization of the payment of debts in a depreciated currency, although debts to him had thus been paid to his great loss, bear witness. He carried the virtues of chivalry into commerce — honor and courage. There is no evidence that he expected success in his mercantile adventures through any other or more dubious expedients than industry, perseverance, self reliance and frugality: and all of these qualities of the merchant, in the letters he has left behind him, he speaks of, and claims to cultivate in his business. As a citizen of the new nation, he interested himself in every public measure projected for the perfecting that edifice, in laying the foundations of which he had participated. Disdaining rather than seeking official position, he was not negligent to inform himself upon those fundamental questions of government and state policy which were then occupying the minds of thoughtful men, in those years of uncertainty, confusion and danger, that succeeded the war, and he proved himself not inapt in giving direction to the political sentiment of the community of which he was a conspicuous and honored member. His letters, written during and after the revolutionary contest, gave evidence of political perspicacity, as well as of his independence of thought and disinterestedness of action. They indicate that he possessed many of the qualifications which belong to politicians of the best, if not of the highest order, and that his state in giving a soldier to the American cause lost a statesman from her councils. In the strictly private relations of life, of companion, friend and relative, of son, husband and parent, he exhibited those amiable traits which excite no envy, but command respect and win affection. In the trying position of a member of a military family, where jealousies are so apt to be engendered, he seems early to have gained, and to the last to have retained, the esteem not only of his commander, but of all his brother officers, and this in an especial degree. He preserved amidst the heats of a controversy which destroyed so many ties, the ancient and beautiful virtue of filial honor, for though separated from his father by differences of political opinion, he never forgot his reverence for him nor sacrificed his affection. His memory is still cherished by a wide circle of relatives and friends, as that of one endowed with the most endearing characteristics of mind and heart; and it is treasured by his descendants as the source of a becoming pride, as the incentive to all that is noble, and as a protection from what is base. He was happy and cheerful in his disposition, hearty and constant in his attachments, fond of society, but found, at last, his chief pleasures in domestic endearments. Withal, he was possessed of a piety which was as sincere as it was exemplary.

> "His life was gentle, and the elements
> So mixed in him, that nature might stand up
> And say to all the world, this was a man."

APPENDIX.

JOURNAL

OF

TENCH TILGHMAN,

SECRETARY OF THE INDIAN COMMISSIONERS, APPOINTED BY CONGRESS
TO TREAT WITH THE SIX NATIONS AT GERMAN FLATS, NEW YORK.

1775, Saturday Augt 5th, left N York at 12 o'clock at night. Wind ahead, worked up with the Tide 10 miles.

Sunday, Augt 6, Wind still ahead and rainy, made sail about 12 o'clock with the Tide, but it beginning to blow very hard about 2 o'clock brought to, having made no more than 4 miles. As we had been up most part of the preceding night, we spent the best part of this day reading and lolling in our Births. Towards evening we called a Council the result of which was to return to New York & remain there till the Wind turned fair, we accordingly hove up and in about an hour and a half arrived there to the satisfaction of us all.

Monday, Augt 7th. Went on board again at 11 o'clock P.M. Wind springing up fair.

Tuesday, Aug. 8th Weighed at 2 o'clock A.M. Wind light and so continued till about 8 o'clock, then a fine breeze which carried us on against tide to Dobb's Ferry, 25 miles from New York; the greatest part of this way is a most romantic prospect. The

Jersey Shore is bounded by a perpendicular Ledge of Rocks about 50 feet in height which come close down to the waters edge, the N York shore is a gradual ascent on which is situated many Gentlemen's Seats an Farm Houses. After taking in the Indian Goods we kept on our Way and about sun set entered the Highlands where the River narrows very considerably. The sailing thro' these mountains by moonlight was a most beautiful sight. Went to bed at 11 o'clock and on Wednesday morning 9th August 6 o'clock A.M., found ourselves at half way Island. The Country now begins to grow less mountainous near the shore, but the distant prospect of the Kats-Kill or Blue Mountain has the most beautiful appearance I ever beheld. The day being misty the Clouds hung low about the Mountains, in some places not seeming more than half way up, in others it appeared like volumes of smoke arising from the Hills. Indeed I thought at first it was owing to burning Brush making Coal or some such matter. Then the breaking out of the sun now and then exhibited a thousand different shades from the darkest to the lightest brown. At 11 o'clock A.M., parted with two very agreeable passengers Mr. Duane & Mr. Livingstone who went on shore at their respective Country Seats. At 5 o'clock P.M. arrived at Albany.

Thursday Aug. 10th Spent in Albany, the Capital of the County of the same name, it consists of about 400 Houses chiefly built after the old low Dutch Fashion. There are two Dutch and one English Churches. On the Hill above the town is a Fort, now gone much to decay. At each end of the town are two very large and handsome houses, one belonging to General Schuyler, the other to M^r^. Ransalear the Lord of the Manor of Ransalear at present a Minor. We found provisions of all kinds very good here, particularly Mutton, Fish they might have from the North River both Rock & perch & Trout from the springs but the people are too lazy to take them.

Friday Augt. 11th. Went from Albany to Schenectady which is 16 Miles this is the most wretched Country I ever saw Nothing but pine Barrens. There are but a house or two upon the Road and not as many Acres of improved Ground. Schenectady is a very pretty Town consisting of between 3 & 400 Houses situated in a fine Bottom upon the Mohawk River a Branch of Hudson's River. This Bottom is so extremely rich and valuable that I am informed it sells from £40 to £80 p Acre. A wealthy Farmer near Schenectady told me that his land had been in Cultivation 120 years successively and that there was not the least appearance of impoverishment. The Land is a rich black Mould and does not seem to have any mixture of Clay.

Saturday Augt 12th. From Schenectady to Fundy's 24 miles, along the Bank of the Mohawk River and for the most part this is the same rich Bottom that begins at Schenectady. The upland is all poor, stony and unsettled. The owners of these invaluable bottoms do not seem to me to deserve them, being to all appearance very bad Farmers. I did not see upon them a stalk of good Indian corn, owing to its being too thick planted, and choacked up with Grass & Weeds which ought not to have been the Case this Year which has been a very dry season. In this stage we passed the Seats of Col°. Guy Johnson, Col°. Clause and Fort Johnson the former residence of L$^{t.}$ William. The Houses of these Gent are very good but scarce any marks of improvement about them. From what I have yet seen of the province of N York it is far behind any other of the Colonies in public spirit, her Roads are narrow, her Bridges loose logs dangerous to pass, and everything bears the Mark of the true situation of the Bulk of the People, A State of Tenancy. We this day met an Indian who informed us that the Deputies from the 5th Nations were on their way to Albany. We therefore sent a messenger to the Mohawk Castles which lay about this place, desiring their head men to meet us in the morning, after seeing them we shall proceed to the German Flats to meet the other Indians on their way. The Mohawks are become a civilized People, they live in good Houses and work their lands to the same advantage that the Whites do. They are vastly diminished in numbers, having not more than 70 men of their tribe.

Sunday Augt 13th this morning, Abichaw the Chief of the Mohawks came to us and after hearing our business, with which he seemed pleased promised to come to us at the Flats to-morrow with more of his Tribe. After Breakfast we set out and as the day was remarkably fine it adde to the pleasure of our Ride thro' such a piece of Country as I believe is not in America. For 32 miles the roads run through the Bottom and along the Bank of the River, the Ground all in cultivation. Wheat Indian Corn, Peas Oats & Grass. What adds to the Beauty is that there are no inclosures, a small path divides each mans property from his Neighbours, and as no Cattle go at large upon these Grounds there is no Inconvenience from want of Fence. 32 miles from our morning stage is Conajohare the upper Mohawk Castle where the small remains of that once Warlike & powerful Nation now dwell in a few miserable Huts. We assembled their Chiefs consisting of 14 or 15 and also desired them to come up to us at the Flats next morning. This they readily agreed to, as they knew a small matter of eating & drinking would be going forward. The Indians have a fine body of Land at this place mostly uncultivated for they do not farm like the people of the lower Castle. The favourite Mistress of the late S^r. William Johnson now lives at Conajohare. But "fallen from her high Estate." She lived with Sr William for 20 years and was treated with as much attention as if she had been his wife. He had several children by her, for all of whom he provided at his Death, he left her a tract of Land and some money, upon which she carries on a small Trade, consisting chiefly I believe in Rum which she sells to the Indians. As she is descended from and connected with the most noble families of the Indians, she was of great use to Sr William in his Treaties with those people. He knew that Women govern the Politics of savages as well the refined part of the World and therefore always kept up a good understanding with the brown Ladies from Conajohare we came on to the German Flats but did not chuse to have an interview with the Indians the same Evening as we knew that if they ever got fooling we should not get rid of them for the Night. Col°. Francis and myself not liking the Appearance of the Beds took up our lodging upon a clean threshing floor where we slept very well and free from the Company that would in all probability have joined us in the House. The German Flats so called from being settled by Germans, are a large body of lowlands running many miles along the south side of the Mohawk River, and two or three miles in depth, which is much deeper than any Bottoms we had yet seen, they tell us they are of a richer quality than any lands we have come over, but that I can hardly think.

Monday Augt. 14th. Early this Morning we sent Messengers across the river to announce our arrival to the Indians The Chief of each Tribe are to pay us a formal visit and after smoking a Pipe or two we shall proceed in a Body to pay our Respects to the Assembly and enform them shortly of our Intention to hold a Treaty at Albany and invite them to it. Being well assured of their ready Compliance. The Great Men arrived about 9 o'clock and after drinking a dram, smoking a pipe, and eating a most immoderate Breakfast of Chocolate, they desired to be informed of the Cause of Meeting. Our Interpreter told them in a few words that M^r. Doer and Col°. Francis were two of the deputies appointed by the Continental Congress to hold a Treaty with the six Nations & the Indians of Canada at Albany, but as the Indians of Canada had not yet been summoned, they desired they would ap-

Journal of Tench Tilghman.

point some of their young men hardy & swift of foot to carry Belts and deliver a Message of Invitation. Their Answer was that they were glad to see us, would call a Council and consider of it   Here I must remark that the Indians never enter into a Controversy upon these occasions, but after hearing what you have to say, answer as above that they will consider what you have said. Neither do they ever talk about the Matter in hand, if they say anything it is about indifferent Subjects, such as enquiring after Acquaintances &c. They very politely desired leave to go home again to their quarters, which we granted after informing them that we would wait upon them in an hour or two. At the appointed time we set out and made as respectable an appearance as we could, having got several of the Neighbouring People to join our Cavalcade. When we arrived at their Quarters we found their Chiefs all in one House to receive us and the men all seated in a Circle in an adjoining Orchard the Women & Children standing at a little distance. Seats were set for us in the area of the Circle. When we entered there was a mutual solemn salutation of How do you do or something of that kind and then a profound silence. Our Interpreter then informed the Body as we had before done the Chiefs of the Nature of our Business, they answered that nothing as yet could be done as the Mohawk Deputies had not come up. We gave them some drink and tobacco and informed them that we should take care to have them well supplied with Bread and Meat. At this they were exceedingly pleased and assured us in general that their Brothers the Americans should find them fast Friends. The Behaviour of the poor Savages at a public Meeting ought to put us civilized people to the Blush. The most profound silence is observed, no interruption of a speaker. When any one speaks all the rest are attentive. We gave them a large Roll of tobacco. Two of their people cut it into pieces of two or three inches, and then distributed them all around. No man rose from his seat to snatch. When drink was served round it was in the same manner, no Man seemed anxious for the Cup. One of them made a speech and set forth the bad effects of drinking at a time of Business and desired that the White people might not have liberty to sell rum to their Young Men. I write this about sunset of a fine evening. The lowlands and Mohawk River below me and two little villages with a Church and Steeples too I assure in each of them.

Tuesday Augt. 15th Last Night the Mohawks came up to us and this morning we were honored with a visit from the favorite of the late S^r. William Johnson. I could not help being affected at the sight of this poor Creature when I reflected on the great Change of her situation in life. For near 20 years he lived in what may be called a state of royalty for no prince was ever as much respected by his subjects as S^r. William was by the different tribes of Indians. They speak of him now with a kind of adoration, they say there never was such a man and never will be such another. Shakespear makes Hamlet speak the same sentiment of his Father. " He was a man take him for all in all whose like I ne'er shall look upon again."

When Molly, for so is this Squaw called, came to us, she saluted us with an air of ease and politeness, she was dressed after the Indian Manner, but her linen and other Cloathes the finest of their kind. One of the Company that had known her before told her she looked thin and asked her if she had been sick, she said sickness had not reduced Her, but that it was the Remembrance of a Loss that could never be made up to her, meaning the death of S^r. William. Upon seeing Mr. Kirkland an Oneida Missionary, she taxed him with neglect in passing by her House without calling to see her. She said there was a time when she had friends enough, but remarked with sensible emotion that the unfortunate and the poor were always neglected. The Indians pay her great respect and I am afraid her influence will give us some trouble, for we are informed that she is working strongly to prevent the meeting at Albany, being intirely in the Interests of Guy Johnson, who is now in Canada, working upon the Cachnawagers, as it is supposed — After framing a short speech to be delivered in full Council, we again proceeded to the Indian Quarters, where we found the Indians ready to receive us, the speech was delivered by Col°. Francis and interpreted to them by Abraham a Mohawk Sachem, to this purpose that they had heard our Voices, but that as they had set long in Council they were tired, but would give an answer tomorrow. They said it was time to take a drink together and bid us remember that the 12 united Colonies were a great Body of people. A modest hint that the drink should be in proportion. But we knew the Consequence too well to indulge.

Wednesday Augt 16th Met the Indians again in Council, who gave us a full answer to our speech of Yesterday, which they complied with every respect, Except that of sending some of their young Men to invite the Indians of Canada. They artfully evaded this by telling us the thing would be impracticable at this time because a Man one of our own Blood was already there endeavouring to draw (pulling strong was their expression) their Minds from us and to prevent their coming down. We asked them who this Man was, they answered they did not chuse to mention his Name, but they had pointed him out sufficiently. Co^{lo}. Guy Johnson was the person pointed at. They delivered us what they call a Path Belt thereby desiring us to make their way clear to Albany & prevent any mischief happening on the way. This we assured them of and parted with wishes of meeting again in a few days at Albany. It is plain to me that the Indians understand their game, which is to play into both hands. They would readily have sent to Canada, but as the Superintendent had taken possession of that ground they did not chuse to interfere with him. They however told us that they knew the minds of the Indians of Canada and that we might make ourselves easy on their accounts.

Thursday Augt 17th we left the Flats and arrived at Albany on Saturday the 19th.

Sunday Augt 20th Hearing that Genl Schuyler was at his seat at Saractoga we determined to pay him a visit and set out this morning. from Albany to Saratoga is 32 miles thro' a country intirely settled since the last War and therefore in no very great improvement tho' pretty thickly settled. The good land is very little in proportion to the bad, being a narrow strip of Bottom along the North River. These Bottoms are very kind to grass to which they seem adapted, they are not of that fine quality, that the Bottoms on the Mohawk River are of. Genl Schuyler has a very fine settlement at Saratogha the Bottom just there is extensive, he has two very fine saw mills and a good grist mill on the Fish Kill which runs into the North River Just by his House and is as fine a Mill Seat as I ever saw. Indeed I did not see another good one in the whole province. We were very genteely entertained by the Genl and his Lady and left them on Monday to return again to Albany. On our way back we met Mr Lynch, Mr Huger and Mr Mutrie going to Ticondiroga and at our Return to Albany had the pleasure to find M^r and Miss Lynch and Mrs Huger there.

Tuesday 22^d Augt. I spent the greatest part of this Morning in a visit to the Ladies where I had the pleasure of being introduced to Miss Ann Schuyler the General's eldest daughter. A very pretty young Lady. A Brunette with dark eyes, and a countenance animated and sensible as I am told she really is. In the afternoon I attended the funeral of old M^r. Doer the father of the Commissioner. This was something in a stile new to me. The Corpse was carried to the ground and interred without any funeral ceremony, tho' Clergymen attended. We then returned to the House of the deceased where we found many Tables set out with Bottles, cool Tankards, Candles, Pipes

& Tobacco. The company set themselves down, lighted their Pipes and handled the Bottles and Tankards pretty briskly. Some of them I think rather too much so. I fancy the undertakers of the funeral had borrowed all the plate of the neighbourhood for the Tankards & Candle Sticks were all silver or plated. Having taken leave of mine host, I called at Genl. Schuyler's seat to pay my compliments to the Genl. his Lady & Daughter. I found none of them at home but Miss Betsy Schuyler the Generals 2^d daughter to whom I was introduced by M^r. Commissary Livingston who accompanied me. I was prepossessed in fav^r of this young Lady the moment I saw her. A Brunette with the most good natured lively dark eyes that I ever saw, which threw a beam of good temper and benevolence over her whole Countenance. M^r. Livingston informed me that I was not mistaken in my Conjecture for that she was the finest tempered Girl in the World. On my Return to Town I waited on my Ladies again to settle the plan of a Jaunt to the Cohoes Falls.

Wednesday 23rd Augt. This morning we set out for the Cohoes in the following order. M^{rs}. Lynch and M^{rs}. Cuyler in a post Chaise. M^{rs}. Huger Miss Betsy Schuyler and M^r. Cuyler in a kind of a Phaeton, Miss Lynch and myself in a Chaise. We arrived at the Cohoes about 11 o'clock. We had not the pleasure of viewing the beautiful Fall, to the best advantage, as the Water (from the lowness of the River for want of Rain) did not run over more than one half of the precipice of rock which I am informed is 74 feet in

Height, the river there is about 400 yards wide we with much difficulty descended the Hills almost perpendicular to the foot of the Falls. My foot once slipped and Miss Lynch who I was supporting and myself had like to have taken a short turn to the bottom. I fancy Miss Schuyler had been used to ramble over and climb grounds of this sort for she disdained all assistance and made herself merry at the distress of the other Ladies. Tho' the water did not fairly shoot over the precipice it tumbled down the rock in a foaming sheet which you may imagine made a wild and most agreeable appearance, having gained the summit of the hill we adjourned to a neighboring farm House where we refreshed ourselves with sherbet Biscuit and Cheese which I had taken care to lay in. We then returned to a House about 6 miles from Albany where we had bespoke dinner, dined and returned to Albany time Enough to be present at an Assembly of the Indians who were got together to receive the welcome of the people of Albany. Col°. Francis told the ladies he would treat them with an Indian dance before our lodgings, we therefore went down there, and I to do my part of the Civilities invited them to take a repast of Sepawn and Milk, which the ladies of Carolina owned was a real treat to them. Two Fires being lighted up in the middle of the street, about 8 o'clock the Indians came down, beating their drum, striking sticks together in Exact time and yelling after their Manner They were almost intirely naked, and after singing some thing in the recicative manner keeping time with their drum and sticks, they would strike out into a Dance around the Fires with the most savage Contortions of Body & limbs. Then upon a signal from one of their Chiefs leave off their dance & return again to their singing which is sometimes in a slow mournful Tone & sometimes more brisk & lively. The dance which followed was always slow or quick as the song had been. I was informed that this song was a recitat of the warlike Actions of the great Men of their Tribes, and that sometimes when worked up by drink, Exercise, and heated imaginations, they would proceed to acts of Enthusiasm. The Dance concluded about ten o'clock and being intirely novel was the more entertaining to the Ladies.

Thursday 24th Augt. we were busy all the morng preparing matters for opening the treaty tomorrow, as a vast deal of Ceremony is to be observed. We dined this day with the Genl. who has a palace of a House and lives like a prince. The ladies from Carolina, the Commissioners and several Genls. from the neighbouring provinces were there. Having occasion to meet some of the Indian Chiefs in the evening, they asked if I had an Indian name being answered in the negative, Tiahogo & the Chief of the Onondagos did me the honor to adopt me into that Tribe and become my father. He christened me Teahokalonde a name of very honourable signification among them, but much the contrary among us. It signifies having large horns. A Deer is the coat of arms, If I may so call it, of the Onondago Tribe, and they look upon horns as an emblem of strength, Virtue and Courage. This name might have made a suspicious man very unhappy, and made him feel his Temples every now and then for the sprouting honours. The christening cost a bowl of punch or two which I believe was the chief motive of the institution.

Friday the 26th Augt. The Treaty was opened with great form, the Pipe of Peace was smoked and Genl. Schuyler delivered the preparatory speech these matters took us up till five o'clock in the afternoon when the meeting adjourned to next day. When Business was over I was admitted into the Onondago Tribe, in presence of all the six nations, and received by them as an adopted son. They told me that in order to settle myself among them they must chuse me a wife, and promised that she should be one of the handsomest they could find. I accepted this proposal with many thanks. Miss Lynch and Miss Betsy Schuyler have promised to stand Brides maids — I expected when I came to Albany to have soon been heartily tired of it, and so I should, but for the arrival of the Carolina Ladies and the coming of Genl. Schuyler's family to town. We now form a very agreeable society. I don't know a greater pleasure than for Acquaintances to meet in a strange place. It seems to be the interest of each to oblige the other and to make the time pass as agreeably as possible. I imagine it is for this reason that the most lasting intimacies are made abroad. At home when we have a number of Acquaintances we call upon one another as it happens to pass away our hour. But always having perhaps but one friend to whom we can apply with Freedom, we attach ourselves to him more closely and thereby come at a more intimate knowledge of his heart and if we find it good one the impression often lasts with our lives.

Saturday 27th Augt. The Treaty opened again about 12 o'clock and continued till about 4 in the afternoon. An Indian Treaty by the by is but dull entertainment owing to the delay and difficulty of getting what you say, delivered properly to the Indians. The Speech is first delivered in short sentences by one of the Commissioners, then an Interpreter tells an Indian what the Commissioner has been saying. After this has been repeated to the Indian he speaks it to the six nations, so that a speech that would not take up twenty minutes in the delivery will from these necessary delays employ us two or three hours. The Speech wrote by the Congress and sent up by the Com^r, gave them a great deal of trouble, as they were obliged to alter it, amend it, and new dress it, and put it into such mode & Figure as would make it intelligible to Indians for in its original form, you might almost as well have read them a Chapter out of Locke or any of our most abstracted reasoners. In the evening we turned out a Bull for the young Indians to hunt and kill after their manner, with arrows, knives, and hatchetts. The Beast was not of the furious spanish breed for he suffered himself to be despatched in a very few minutes without ever turning upon his assailants. We then put up two laced Hats and a silver arm Band to be run for. I think I have seen white men who would have outstripped these Champions, as their mode of running seemed more calculated for a long distance than for swiftness, their strides are long and strong. Their Race I think was about a quarter of a mile. Tomorrow M^r. Kirkland promises us a sermon where we shall have an opportunity of hearing the Oneida ladies sing. As these sports were in a field near the Gen^{ls}. House we drank Coffee and spent the evening there not in the formal but in the agreeable accidental manner. There is something in the behaviour of the Genl. his lady & daughters that makes you acquainted with them instantly. I feel myself as easy and free from restraint at his seat as I am at Cliffdon, where I am always at a second home.

Sunday 28th Augt. In the afternoon we were favoured with Mr Kirkland's Indian sermon whether it was a good or a bad one I dont know but if I might judge from the translation of some of what he thought the most striking parts, I have no great opinion of his pulpit oratory. I was disappointed in the singing. The voices of the Indians taken distinctly were well enough, but by endeavoring to make out Tenor, Treble and Base they spoilt the whole. The men & women sung one anthem in two parts which they performed pleasingly enough. The fault of the women was that they always strained their voices too high. By an express just arrived from Ticonderoga I find that I shall be robbed of a very agreeable part of my Albany acquaintance, as the Genl is obliged to set off immediately for Ticonderoga and his Lady and Family for Saratogha. I will wait on them in the morning and bid them adieu.

Monday 29th Augt went out to breakfast with the Genl. and to take my leave of him and the Ladies. I found the girls up and ready for their march breakfast was on the Table and down I sat among them like an old Acquaintance, tho' this is only the seventh day since my introduction. It would be seven years before I could be as intimate with half the World. But there is so much frankness & freeness in this Family that a man must be dead to every feeling of Familiarity who is not familiarized the first hour of his being among them. Nature has given them at Albany what the Tour of Europe could not give to Mr Startope with all Lord Ches—— 'Assistance. They would not let me leave them without some mark of kindness, and therefore loaded me with Grapes which they plucked fresh from the vines themselves. About 12 o'clock we renewed the Businiss of the Treaty and by 4 in the afternoon got thro' all that we have to say to them except some trifling matters. The day after to-morrow we shall have their answer. And I hope the day after that we shall be near turning our Backs upon Albany. Our Carolina friends go away tomorrow and then it will be a solitude indeed. I sat near an hour this evening hearing a parcel of Stockbridge Indian Girls sing Hymns. They far excell the Oneidas in this, and add to the account that they are pretty and extremely cleanly they speak tolerable English too, so that I believe I must make an Acquaintance among them when my fair Country women are all gone, for I think they are superior to any of the Albanians, a Miss Ransolaer excepted who is the Belle of the Town

and therefore a little of the Coquette. I will have a
Tete a Tete with her before I go. And give her a
place in my Journal.

Tuesday a rainy day which suited my Businiss very
well as I had much to do within doors and the
weather was not inviting without. We dined with a
shoal of Connecticut Gentlemen, who of all the people
I ever saw the most uncouth in their Manner. I got
rid of them as soon as I decently could and flew for
relief to the quarters of my Carolina friends. Thanks
to the Winds for detaining them here all day. Shall
I be illnatured if I pray for adverse winds till we are
ready to go. I think not it can be no great disadvantage to them and will be of infinite pleasure and convenience to me. Surely then Father Aeolus may
grant my request without much detriment to them.
It will be only raising his pipes one note higher when
we are all on board, and making up for lost time by
the Briskness of the gale. I have invoked the God of
the Winds now I invoke the God of sleep. Be propitious both.

Wednesday. My prayers are not answered. The
wind sets fair and I have this moment seen the embarkation of My Carolina Friends. Albany I care
not how soon I bid thee farewell. But for the interposition of a few christian like people I should have
cursed thee long ago. The town is crowded with
Indians & Soldiers, it is hard say which is the most
irregular and Savage. The former are mutinous for
want of liquor the latter for want of pay, without
which they refuse to march. The Troops raised in

and about New York are a sad pack. They are mostly old disbanded Regulars and low lived foreigners. The companies raised in the country are hale hearty young men and seem fit to undergo hardships. From the accounts Genl Schuyler gave us of the state of his Army, I tremble for him in his Expedition ag^t S^t. Johns he wants almost everything necessary for the equipment of an army. He complains much of the Dilatoriness of the York Committee. His great dependance is upon the Neutrality of the Canadians, if they do not assist Gov. Carelton, Schuyler has numbers sufficient to rout badly disciplined and accoutred as they are — Well tho' the God of the Winds would not be propitious, the God of the Tides has laid an Embargo upon the Carolina Genteels. M^r. Lynch has just come up and tells me that the sloop sticks fast upon the over fall a shoal about 3 miles below We have dispatched a Carriage to bring back the Ladies who must now wait another Tide. We dined this day with M^r. Commissioner Doer. We had not only a plentiful but a good dinner well cooked & served up. After it a handsome desert of Fruits Peaches, Pears, Plumbs, Grapes &c. Mr Doer gave us some of the red or swamp plumb which he transplanted into his garden. This has increased them vastly in size and I think them not only a very beautiful but a very good Fruit. Then Brother Richard we had Madeira and plenty of it. That cost our Host £32 stirling and has been 8 years in his cellar. It was most excellent. They drink far better Madeira in this province than in ours. In their public Houses a great distance from N York their Madeira is unadulterated and as good if not better than you generally meet with in our best Taverns in Phila^d. I wish I could say as much of their Butter. I have not greased my teeth with a Bit of right good since I left Phila^d. except in the Jerseys.

Thursday 31st Augt. We this day received a full answer to the speech delivered to the Indians on Saturday and Monday. It is amazing with what exactness these people recollect all that has been said to them. The speech which we delivered took up nine or ten pages of folio Paper, when they came to answer they did not omit a single head and on most of them repeated our own words, for it is a Custom with them to recapitulate what you have said to them and then give their Answer. They are thorough bred politicians. They know the proper time of making demands. They reaped up several old Grievances and demanded Redress, well imagining that nothing would be denied them at this time. We expected that this would have finished the Treaty, but soon matters turned up in the Course of the Indian speech which will oblige the Commissioners to meet them again tomorrow but it will be short.

Friday 1st Sep^t. 'Tis finished, we have taken leave of their Majesty's if the six nations who are to receive their presents in the morning and return from whence they came. We have embarked our Cavalry and Baggage and if the winds set fair in the morning hoist sail and farewell Albany. If foul, embark again and take our Land-Tacks or Boards. Who should bless my eye sight this evening but good natured agreeable Betsy Schuyler just returned from Saratogha. I declare I was as glad to see her as if she had been ever so old an Acquaintance, I had the farther pleasure too of being introduced to Miss Ransolaer who is a Relation and with whom she lodges. Miss Ransolaer is pretty, quite young and fond of joked about her humble servants. As I had made myself master of a good deal of her private history. I could touch upon such matters as I knew would be agreeable to her. I lamented that my short stay in Albany would so soon deprive me of so agreeable an Acquaintance and a deal more of such common place stuff. This was mere Compliment to her, but I told Miss Schuyler so with truth; for in Truth I am under infinite obligations to the kindness of her and her family.

Saturday 2^d Sep^t. Left Albany on board Capt. Lansings sloop, the wind fair but very light. We got down almost as far as Kinder Hook by 5 P.M., and there came to anchor. The Capt. & myself diverted ourselves with fishing and in two hours caught between 4 & 5 doz. very pretty white perch. We landed and got Milk, Fruit & Vegetables. It is stark Calm and I fear a southerly wind to-morrow.

Sunday morning 10 o'clock all bustle — what's the matter Capt. A fine N E wind and we are getting under sail — very well good-bye to you then. 8 o'clock A.M. Wind still fresh and fair and we trimming it along against tide. The next Tide will carry us almost down to N York if the wind continues. About 12 P.M. the wind began to shift and be squally, which made it very disagreeable especially to our poor Horses who were every now and then upon their broadsides.

About sun set we brought to again and lay till next morning.

Monday 3rd Sep^t Wind still ahead and likely to continue so, we beat it down to Newburgh just at the entrance of the Highlands and finding no likelyhood of fair weather, disembarked our cavalry and proceeded by land to one Smiths 14 miles thro' the Mountains.

Tuesday 4 Sep^t We left Smiths early in the morning as we intended to reach Hackensack that Night which is 40 miles and bad Road. Tho' we were prepared for bad Road we found it worse than we expected, the whole way till within 14 miles of Hackensack thro' the Gap of the Mountains It put me in mind of Don Quixote's rambles thro'

COL. TILGHMAN'S DIARY

OF THE

SIEGE OF YORKTOWN.

22^d Sept. 1781. Part of the advanced Fleet with the French Grenadiers and Chasseurs and American light troops came up to College Creek.

23^d. Remainder of the Fleet came up — American Troops debarked as fast as they arrived and ordered to encamp near the landing. Genl. Lincoln is of opinion that the large transports with the French line and remainder of the American are in James River — French Grenadiers and Chasseurs encamped below the Capitol, Olney & Hazen's Reg^t. and some Companies of the 15 Infantry an Jersey line not yet arrived.

24. Olney's and Hazen's Reg^t. arrived safe in the flat Boats. Transports with the French Troops arrived also — Boats with part of the 15 Infantry and Jersey line were driven on shore in the Bay — Vessels sent to bring them off. American troops encamp below the Capitol.

25. French Troops debarking.

26, 27th, debarking.

28. The army moved down before York, without any interruption from the Enemy.

29. Spent in reconnoitering Enemy's position.

30. It was found this morning that the enemy had evacuated pidgion quarter and all their exterior line.

1st, 2d, 3d, 4th October throwing up Redoubts to cover our approaches and bringing Cannon & Stores from Trebetts landing upon James River.

5 & 6th, employed as above. 6 in the afternoon Col. Scammel died of his wounds the 6th at night the Trenches were opened between 5 & 600 yards from the Enemy's works and the 1st parallel Run — commencing abt the Centre of the Enemy's works opposite the secretary's House and running to the right to York River. The parallel supported by 4 Redoubts — These approaches are directed agt the 4 works on the Enemy's left — The Enemy kept up a pretty brisk fire during the night but as our working parties were not discovered by them, their shot were in a wrong direction. This same night Mr. St. Simons began to throw up a work upon the left against a detached Redoubt of the enemy on this side the mouth of the Creek. A false attack *was made* in the night upon the left to *draw* the Enemy's attention that way only one officer and one man upon the Right were wounded of Marquis St Simons commd one officer wounded and 15 privates killed and wounded.

7th. Employed completing the 1st Parallel and the Redoubts upon it.

The night of the 7th four new works were commenced advanced of the 1st parallel, in Mt. scarce any annoyance from the enemy. 1 Man of ours killed by the firing of one patrole upon the other and 1 man had his

The Siege of Yorktown.

foot shot off — 2 men wounded in the french Trenches.

8. Still employed completing the advanced Redoubts — fire of the Enemy very slack — this night one American killed — 1 wounded 1 French killed — 4 badly wounded.

9^t. In the afternoon Marquis St Simon's Battery of 4–12 pounders and 6 Howitzers opened as also did the American Battery on the right of six-10 and 24 pounders and 2 Howitzers and 2 mortars, the Fire of the enemy extremely slack and no mischief *done* to us.

10^t. The Grand French Battery of 10–18 and 24 pounders and 6 mortars opened and another of 4–18 ps — as did Machins Battery of 4–18 ps and one of 2 mortars — The embrasures of the enemys Works considerably damaged and by report of M^r. Secretary Nelson our shells did a good deal of damage. In the evening the Charon of 44 Guns was set on fire by a Ball and burnt — Her Guns and Stores had been previously taken out.

11th. Fire from all the Batteries continued — 2 transport Vessels fired by hot shot and burnt. The French Bomb Battery of 6 mortars opened — The night of the 11th the 2^d parallel was opened within 300 yards of the enemy's Works with scarce any annoyance only one man killed and three or four wounded.

12th. Employed in compleating 2^d Parallel.

13th. Employed as above.

14th. d°. The 14 just after dark the two Works on the left of the enemy's line were carried by assault — that on the extreme left by the L^t. Infantry under the command of Marquis de la Fayette — the next to it, by the French Grenadiers under the command of Baron Vumenel — the troops behaved with the utmost bravery, they entered the Works under the Enemy's fire with fixed Bayonets without firing a shot. A Maj^r. two Captains and three Subs and 67 privates were made prisoners. A false attack was made on the Enemy's right about half an hour before the real attack. We had about 40 officers and men killed and wounded. The French about 90.

15th. Compleating the 2 parallel and constructing Batteries upon it — the night of the 15th the enemy made a sortie — They entered one of the French and one of the American unfinished Batteries and spiked 6 Cannon with the points of Bayonets, which made them to be unspiked with ease, they 7 or 8 dead and 6 prisoners — the French had four officers wounded and twenty men killed and wounded — We had one Sarj^t. mortally wounded.

16th. Compleating 2^d parallel — Several Batteries upon it opened, which galled the Enemy much.

17th. In the morning L^d. Cornwallis put out a letter requesting that 24 Hours might be granted to Commissioners to settle terms of Capitulation for the surrender of the posts of York and Gloster. The General answered that two Hours only would be allowed to him to send out his terms in writing. He accordingly sent them out, generally as follow, that the Garrisons should be prisoners of War, the German & British Soldiers to be sent to England and Germany. The Customary terms of it and presentation of private property — &c. The General answered on the 18th, that the terms of sending the Troops to England and Germany were inadmissible. That the honors should be the same as those granted at Charlestown — private property preserved &c. His Lordship closed with all the terms except those of acceding to the same honors as those granted at Ch^s Town. However the Comm^{rs}. met— on our part L^t. Col^o. Laurens & Viscount Noiailles — on the part of the British Col^n. Dundas, Maj^r. Ross.

CORRESPONDENCE.

Mount Vernon 23ᵈ Mar — 73.
Dear Sir,
I expect Govʳ Eden and some gentlemen from Maryland here this afternoon — If you are disengaged, I should be glad if you would come down and stay with us a day or two, or as long as they remain
with

Yʳ. most obedᵗ. Servᵗ.
To James Tilghman Esq.   Gº. WASHINGTON
    At Alexandᵃ.

Mount Vernon May 10ᵗʰ 1786
Sir — Being at Richmond when your favor of the 22ⁿᵈ ultº came to this place is the reason of its having lain so long unacknowledged. I delayed not a moment after my return to discharge the balance of your deceased Brother's acct. against me to Mʳ. Watson according to your request.

As there were few men for whom I had a warmer friendship or greater regard than for your Brother — Colonel Tilghman — when living; so, with much truth I can assure you that there are none whose death I could more sincerely have regretted. — And I pray you & his numerous friends to permit me to mingle my sorrows with theirs on this unexpected and melancholy occasion and that they would accept my compliments of condolence on it.

I am Sir Yʳ most obedᵗ Hᵇˡᵉ Servᵗ.
Mr. Thᵒˢ R. Tilghman   Gº. WASHINGTON
    Baltimore

Head Q^{rs}. Newburgh
9th of July 1782.

My Dear Sir

' Till your letter of the 28th ult° arrived (which is the first from you, & the only direct acc^t. of You, since we parted at Philadelphia)— We have had various conjectures about you — Some thought you were *dead* — others that you were *married* — and all that you had *forgot* us.— Your letter is not a more evident contradiction of the first and last of these suppositions than it is a tacit confirmation of the Second; and as none can wish you greater success in the prosecution of the Plan you are upon than I do, so believe me sincere, when I request you to take your own time to accomplish it, or any other business you may have on hand — at the same time I must be allowed to add, that you have no friend that wishes more to see you than I do.—

I have been in constant expectation ever since my arrival at this place, of a summons to meet Count Rochambeau at Philadelphia to settle a plan for the ensuing Campaign — The non arrival of the dispatches from his Court has hitherto prevented it — but the absolute necessity) to avoid delay after they do arrive)— has induced me to propose a meeting at all events, that we may settle such hypothetical plans as will facilitate our operations, without waiting an interview after the dispatches shall arrive.

I shall know the result of this proposition in the course of a few day's, as my dispatches left this the 24th ult°

We have nothing New in this Quarter — Sir Guy, gives strong assurances of the pacific disposition of His most gracious Majesty — by Land — Sir (that is to be) Digby, gives proofs, if he is dificient in assurances, of His said Excellent Majesty's kind intention of Capturing every thing that swims on the face of the *Waters;* and of his humane design of suffocating all those who are found thereon, in

Prison Ships, if they will not engage in his *service* — This, to an American, whose genious is not susceptable of refined ideas, would appear somewhat inconsistent; but to the expanded mind of a Briton they are perfectly reconcilable.— Whether they are right, or wrong time must determine.

I am just returned from a Visit to our Northern Posts, in which Albany, Schenectady, Saratoga, the   and the Fields of Burgoyne were visited — Mrs. Washington who sets out this day for Mount Vernon, thanks you for your kind remembrance of her — she wishes you, as I do, as much happiness as you can do yourself,

   Sincerely & affect^{ly}
    I am — Dr Sir
     Y^r Obed^t Servt
      G^o Washington

Lt Col^o Tilghman.

    Philadelphia, May 18 — 1784
My dear Sir

I pray you to accept the enclosed [1] (if a member of the Society of Cincinnatti) — I sent for one for each of my aids de Camp

   In haste
    I am very affect^{ly} Y^{rs}
     G^o Washington

Col^o Tilghman

    Newburgh 10th Jan 7. 1783
My Dear Sir,

I have been favored with your letters of the 22^d & 24th of last month from Philadelph^a; & thank you for the trouble you have had with my small commissions.— I have sent Mr Ritterhouse the glass of such spectacles as

---

[1] A badge or order of the Society of the Cincinnati, at present in the possession of Oswald Tilghman, Esq.

suit my eyes, that he may know how to grind his Christals.—

Neither Du portail nor Gouvoir are arrived at this place.—To the latter, I am refered by the Marq^s la Fayette for some matters which he did not chuse to commit to writing.— The sentim^{nt} however which he has delivered (with respect to the negociations for Peace) accord precisely with the ideas I have entertained of this business ever since the secession of Mr Fox.—viz—that no peace would be concluded before the meeting of the British Parliament.—And that, if it did not take place within a month afterwards, we might lay our acc^t for one more Campaign — *at least*

The obstinacy of the King, & his unwilling to acknowledge the Independency of this Country, I have ever considered as the greatest obstacles in the way of a Peace.— Lord Shelburne, who is not only at the head of the Administration, but has been introducing others of similar sentiments to his own — has declared, that nothing but *dire necessity* should ever force the measure.— of this necessity, men will entertain different opinions.—Mr Fox, it seems, thought the period had arrived some time ago; and yet Peace is not made — nor will it, I conceive; if the influence of the Crown can draw forth fresh supplies from the Nation, for the purpose of carrying on the War. By the meeting of Parliament, Lord Shelburne would have been able to ascertain two things — first, the best terms on which G. Britain could obtain Peace.— Secondly, the ground on which he himself stood.— If he found it slippery & that the voice of the people was for pacific measures — he would then, have informed the Parliament that, after many months spent in Negociation — such were the best terms he could obtain — and that the alternative of accepting them — or preparing vigorously for the prosecution of the War, was submitted to their consideration (being an extraordinary case) and decision.— A little time therefore, If I have formed a just opinion of the matter, will disclose the result of it — consequently, we shall either soon have Peace, or not the most agreeable prospect of War, before us — as it appears evident to me, that the States *generally*, are sunk into the most profound lethargy, while some of them are running *quite* retrogade.— The King of G. B. by his letters Patent (which I have seen) has authorized Mr Oswald to treat with any Commissioner or Com^rs from the *United States* of America, who shall appear with proper powers — This, certainly, is a capital point gained.— It is at least breaking ground on *their* part, — And I daresay proved a bitter pill to Royalty; that, it was indispensably necessary to answer one of the points above mentioned, as the American Commissioners would enter in *no business* with Mr Oswald till his Powers were made to suit their purposes.— Upon the whole, I am fixed in an opinion that Peace or a pretty long continuance of the War, will have been determined before the adjournment for the Hollidays; and as it will be the middle or last of February before we shall know the result, time will pass heavily on in this dreary mansion — where we are, at present, fast locked in frost & snow.—

Nothing new has happened in this quarter since you left it, except the abuse of me in a New York Paper for having given *false information* to the Count de Vergennes, which (says the writer) was the occasion of the insinuation in *his Letter to me* of a want of British Justice — I have not seen the Paper but am told the author of the piece is quite in a passion at my want of ingenuity.— And ascribes the release of Captn Asgill to a *peremptory order* from the Court of France (in whose service he places me) notwithstanding the soft and complaisant language of the French Minister's Letter.

Mrs Washington has received the Shoes you ordered for

her, & thanks you for your attention to her request — I receive with great sensibility & pleasure, your assurances of affection & regard. It would be but a renewal of what I have often repeated to you, that there are few men in the world to whom I am more attached by inclination than I am to you.— With the Cause, I hope — most devoutly hope,— there will soon be an end to my Military Services — When, as our places of residence will not be far apart, I shall never be more happy than in your Company at Mt Vernon. I shall always be glad to hear from, and keep up a corrispondence with you.—

Mrs Washington joins me in every wish that can tend to your happiness — Humphrys & Walker, who are the only Gentlemen of the Family that are with me at present — will speak for themselves.— If this finds you at Baltimore, I pray my respects to Mr Carroll & Family.— with the greatest esteem and regard

I am — Dear Sir
Yr most Obed and
Affect Hubl Servt
G^o Washington

Rocky Hill Octr. 2^d, 1783.

Dear Sir:

The Chev^r. de la Luzerne, hearing me the other day enquire after Claret, informed me that he had a quantity of it at Baltimore — more than he wanted — & would spare me some. — I am, in consequence, to have two or three Hhds of this Stock. I requested him to direct his corrispondent at that place, to commit them to your care, on the supposition that you are a resident of Baltimore, and I have to beg your attention to them accordingly. —

As you know how liable Liquors are to be adulterated by common Boatmen, or common   ; an that it is the *quality only* which constitutes the value, I perswade myself you will put this wine into the charge of some person who will be responsible for the safe transportation of it,— The Chev^r assures me that it is old wine, and of the first quality.— I hope to drink a Glass of it with you at Mount Vernon 'ere long; and for this, and other reasons, wish it may precede my arrival, at that place— accompany it, if you please, with a line to Mr Washington.

Why have you been so niggardly in communicating your change of condition to us? — or to the world ? — By dint of enquiries we have *heard* of your Marriage ; but have scarcely got a *confirmation* of it yet.— On the presumption however that it is so, I offer you my warmest congratulation & best wishes for the enjoyment of many happy years ; in both which Mrs Washington joins me very cordially.

She is on the eve of setting out for Virginia before the Weather and roads get bad.— I shall follow as soon as the Definite Treaty arrives — or New York is evacuated by our Newly acquired friends.— Of the first there is little said — of the latter a great deal, but scarcely the same thing by any two who come from there.— The general opinion however is, that they will be gone by the last of this month.

Present Mrs Washington's & my compliments to your Lady and Mrs. Carroll, and be assured that with great truth and affection

I am. Dr Sir
Y^r Obed^t Servt
G. WASHINGTON

Mount Vernon 14th July 1785.

Dear Sir,

A Nephew of mine, brother to the young Gentleman who studied law under Mr Wilson in Phil^a, is inclined to enter into a Mercantile walk of life ; and his Father is desirous he should do so.— He has just completed a regular education — is about 20 years of age, sober, serious, & sensible — and I am told remarkably prudent, & assiduous in the execution of whatever he takes in hand.

This is the character he bears, personally, I know little of him.—

I have expressed a wish to his father that he might be placed under your care, and it is highly pleasing to him.— let me ask then, my dear Sir; if it would be convenient for you to take him into your Counting House, and immediately under your eye?— If I had not conceived (from the character he bears) that he would do you no discredit, but may where he is qualified, subserve your views in Trade while he is promoting your own, I do assure you that I would be among the last persons who would propose the measure to you.

If you incline to receive him, be so good as to let me know on what terms, and the requisites to be complied with on his part, as soon as convenient.— Mrs Washington joins very cordially in compliments of congratulation to you and Mrs Tilghman on the encrease of your family.— With the usual esteem and regard I am, Dr Sir Y^r

Affec^t Hble Servt

Tench Tilghman Esqr.   G^o WASHINGTON

Mount Vernon June 2^d, 1785.

Dear Sir,

As your letter of the 30th ult^o did not reach me until late this afternoon, and the Post goes from Alex^a at 4 O'clock in the morning, I have scarcely a moment (being also in company) to write you a reply.—I was not sufficiently explicit in my last. The terms upon which M^r. Falconer came to this Country are too high for my finances — and (to you, my dear Sir, I will add) numerous expences.— I do not wish to reduce his (perhaps well founded) expectations; but it behooves me to consult my own means of complying with them.

I had been in hopes, that a young man of no great expectations might have begun the world with me for about fifty or sixty pounds —, but for one qualified in all respects to answer my purposes, I would have gone as far as seventy-five — more would rather distress me.—

My purposes are these — To write letters agreeably to what shall be dictated.— Do all other writing which shall be entrusted to him.— Keep Acct^s.— Examine, arrange, & properly methodize my Papers, which are in great disorder.— Ride, at my expence, to do such business as I may have in different parts of this, or the other States, if I should find it more convenient to send, than attend myself, to the execution thereof. And which was not hinted at in my last to inetiate two little children (a girl of six & a boy of 4 years of age, descendants of the deceased M^r. Austin, who live with me, and are very promesing) in the first rudiments of education.— This to both parties, would be mere amusement, because it is not my wish that the Children should be confined.— If M^r. Falconer should incline to accept the above stipend in addition to his board, washing and mending,— and *you* (for I would rather have *your opinion* of the Gentleman than the *report* of a thousand others in his favor) upon a close investigation of his character, Temper & moderate political tenets (for supposing him an English man, he may come with the prejudices, & doctrines of his Country) the sooner he comes, the better my purpose would be promoted.—

If I had had time, I might have added more, but to you it would have been unnecessary.— You know my wants.— You know my disposition — and you know what kind of a man would suit them.— In haste I bid you adieu — with assurances of great regard & sincere friendship,

I am — D Sir
Y^r Affect^o H^{ble} Servt

Tench Tilghman Esqr G^o Washington.

Mount Vernon 29th Augt 1785

Dear Sir,

Your favor of the 25th in answer to mine of the preceeding week, came safely. At the time I wrote that letter, I was uninformed of the circumstances which you have since made me acquainted with.—However, you will be at no loss from the contents of it, to discern that it was *Bargains* I had in contemplation; and which, from the quantity of Goods at Market — Scarcity of Cash, according to News paper Acc^{ts} distress of the Trade — & the mode of selling, I thought might probably be obtained;—but if I am mistaken therein, I shall content myself with the few marked articles, or such of them as can be had cheap.— Fine Jacconet Muslin (apron width) is what Mrs Washington wants, and ab^t 5 or 7 yards would be sufficient.— As the arrack is in large Casks & new, I decline taking any.—

If M^r O'Donnell should feel an inclination to make this part of Virginia a visit, I shall be happy in seeing him — and if instead of giving him a *letter* of introduction you should change the mode and introduce him in your own Propria Personæ it would add much to the pleasure of it.— Before your letter was received, from my reading, or rather from an imperfect recollection of what I had read I had conceived an idea that the Chinese though droll in shape and appearance, were yet white.

I am glad to hear that my Packet to Mrs Smith had got safely to hand as there were papers of consequence transmitted.— I expect some other documents for my Law Suit in the course of a few days from our attorney Genl (Edm^d Randolph Esqr) which I shall take the liberty of inclosing to you to be forwarded to Mrs Smith — and as I seem to be in the habit of giving you trouble, I beg the favor of you to cause the inclosed letter to be delivered to Mr Rawlins — I leave it open for your perusal — My reason for it is, that thereby seeing my wants, you would be so obliging as to give me your opinion of Mr Rawlins with respect to his abilities and diligence as a work man — whether he is reckoned moderate or high, in his charges — and whether there is much call, at this time, for a man of his profession at Baltimore — for, on this, I presume, his high or moderate terms will greatly depend.

M^{rs}. Washington joins me in best respects to Mrs Tilghman and yourself, and thanks you for the obliging assurance of chusing the articles wanted, perfect of their kind.

With great esteem & regard
I am — Dear Sir
Y^r. Affect friend &
Obed^t. H^{ble} Servt.
G^o Washington

P. S. Since writing the foregoing, Mrs Washington has requested me to add that if any fine thin Handkerchiefs, with striped or worked borders are to be had, she would be glad to get six of them. G. W.

Tench Tilghman, Esqr.

Mount Vernon 5th June 1786.

Dear Sir,

I have just had the honour to receive your favour of the 26th ult^o .—

Of all the numerous acquaintances of your lately deceased son, & amidst all the sorrowings that are mingled on that melancholy occasion, I may venture to assert (that excepting those of his nearest relatives) none could have felt his death with more regret than I did, because, no one entertained a higher opinion of his worth, or had imbibed sentiments of greater friendship for him than I had done. That you, Sir, should have felt the keenest anguish for this loss, I can readily conceive,— the ties of parental affection united with those of friendship could not fail to have produced this effect. It is however a dispensation, the wisdom of which is inscrutable, and amidst all your grief, there is this consolation to be drawn;— that while living, no man could be more esteemed, and since dead, none more lamented than Col°. Tilghman.—

As his correspondence with the com^{tee} of New York is not connected with any transactions of mine, so, consequently, it is not necessary that the Papers to which you allude should compose part of my public documents; but if they stand single, as they exhibit a trait of his public character, and like all the rest of his transactions will, I am persuaded, do honor to his understanding and probity, it may be desirable in this point of view, to keep them alive by mixing them with mine; which, undoubtedly, will claim the attention of the Historian.— Who, if I mistake not, will, upon an inspection of them, discover the illiberal ground on which the charge mentioned in the extract of the letter you did me the honor to inclose me is founded.— That a calumny of this kind had been reported, I knew;— I had laid my acct. for the calumnies of annonymous scribblers; but I never before had conceived that such an one as is related, could have originated with, or have met the countenance of Capt Asgill; whose situation often filled me with the keenest anguish.

I felt for him on many accts.; and not the least, when, viewing him as a man of honor & sentiment, how unfortunate it was for him that a wretch who possessed neither, should be the means of causing in him a single pang or a disagreeable sensation.— My favourable opinion of him however is forfeited, if, being acquainted with these reports, he did not immediately contradict them.— That I could not have given countenance to the insults which *he says* were offered to his person, especially the *grovelling* one of erecting a Gibbet before his prison window, will I expect, readily be believed, when I explicitly declare that I never heard of a single attempt to offer an insult, and that I had every reason to be convinced, that, he was treated by the officers around him, with all the tenderness and every civility in their power — I would fain ask Captn Asgill how he could reconcile such belief (if his mind had been seriously impressed with it) to the continual indulgencies and procrastinations he had experienced? — He will not I presume deny that, he was admitted to his parole within ten or twelve miles of the British lines: — if not to a formal parole, to a confidence yet more unlimited — by being permitted for the benefit of his health and recreation of his mind, to ride, not only about the cantonment, but into the surrounding country for many miles with his friend and companion Maj. Gordon, constantly attending him. Would not these indulgencies have pointed a military character to the pourtrait from whence they flowed? Did he conceive that discipline was so lax in the American army as that *any* officer *in it* would have granted these liberties to a Person confined by the express order of the Commander in Chief, unless authorized to do so by the same authority? and to ascribe them to the interference of Count de Rochambeau, is as void of foundation as his other conjectures; for I do not recollect that a sentence ever passed between that General and me, directly, or indirectly, on the subject. I was not without suspicions after the final liberation and return of Capt. Asgill to New York that his mind had been improperly impressed or that he was defective in politeness. The treatment he had met with, in my conception, merited an acknowledgment — None however was offered, and I never sought for the cause.

This concise acct. of the treatment of Capt. Asgill is given from a hasty recollection of the circumstances.— If I had had time, and it was essential, by unpacking my papers and recurring to authentic files, I might have been more pointed and full.— It is in my power at any time to convince the unbiased mind that my conduct through the whole of the transaction was neither influenced by passion — guided by inhumanity or under the control of any interference whatsoever.— I essayed everything to save the innocent and bring the guilty to punishment, with what success the impartial world must and hereafter certainly will decide

With very great esteem and regard
I have the honor to be
Dear Sir Your most obed servt.

James Tilghman Esqr }   G^o. WASHINGTON

Letter of Col. T. Tilghman to the Hon. Matthew Tilghman apprising him of his engagement to his daughter.

Chester Toun 10^t June 1782

D^r. Sir

I should not only deem myself unworthy a continuance of that friendship and regard, of which you have given me so many obliging proofs, but I sh^d think myself justly chargeable with a breach of that confidence which you reposed in me, by the kindest admittance into your family, were I to endeavour or even wish, to conceal from you, a matter the most interesting to me, of any which has occurred in the course of my life, and which, I conceive, can be no less so to you, in as much as the happiness & welfare of a daughter an ornament to her sex, may intimately connected with it — From what I have premised, I presume you cannot doubt my meaning — I will therefore beg leave candidly to lay before you every step which I have ventured to take previous to this declaration and I cannot but hope whatever may be your determination that you will acquit me of having acted hitherto inconsistently wlth the principles of a man of the strictest honor.— I may date the commencement of my acquaintance with my lovely Cousin, from the visit I had the pleasure of making you three years ago. Her many engaging qualities did not fail, at that time, to make an impression upon me which has never been effaced; but involved as we then were in a contest, the issue of which was at least precarious (and on which I had determined to stake my life and fortune) I thought it most prudent then to stifle my feelings and to await a more favorable opportunity of making known to her the fondest wishes of my heart, should I be happy enough to find her, at some future day, in a condition to listen to my addresses — That time at length arrived — The aspect of public affairs encouraged me, to hope that our troubles were not far from an end — a nearer and more intimate acquaintance with my Cousin seemed to confirm my regard for her, but an obstacle which then presented itself, and which may still exist for some time, determined me yet barely to explain the motives of my conduct and behaviour which I was convinced could not but appear particular, to a Lady of my Cousin's good sense and penetration. That obstacle was a want of sufficiency of Fortune to maintain her in the stile in which she had been brought up and from which no man had a right I conceived, reasonably, to expect her to descend — I accordingly took an occasion of entering upon the subject fully and freely with her, at the same time assuring her that I could not upon just terms ever expect an answer much less would I wish to draw her into any engagements that I should never mention the matter again untill I could with propriety propose it to her Friends — and begged her to believe, that nothing could have drawn this confession from me, but a conviction that my conduct demanded some explanation, and a secret hope, that should she possibly entertain any sentiments in my favor, they might have their due operation should other offers be made to her in my absence — If I have been at all blameable, it has been in the last instance should you think I have, appeal but for a moment to your own Heart, and I am convinced I shall stand excused — In this manner matters rested, until a few days before I left Talbot; and I should not have thought perhaps myself under an obligation of making an application of this nature to you 'till some time hence, unless I had found it reported from a variety of Quarters, that I there was actually engaged between my Cousin & myself: this I know must naturally reach your Ears, and as I was conscious there were some grounds for just reports, I clearly saw the indelicacy and impropriety of making you, who ought to be the first, the last acquainted with the truth. I took the liberty of expressing my opinion to my cousin, and had the satisfaction of finding her ideas correspond with mine. Your absence at the time of taking this resolution prevented the communication from being a personal one. I would have preferred it on many accounts to the present mode. I think I have neither omitted or misrepresented any circumstance of which you ought to be informed. Had I no other tie the fear of appearing by permission of the truth, despicable in the eyes of a Woman too replete with every Virtue to overlook such a meaness and whose good opinion I should not forfeit for the World, would be a sufficient security against my making any attempt to deceive you — It now remains for me to be more explicit on the subject of my present and future prospects as to fortune — previous to the war, I had principally by my own industry acquired so much as would with a continuance of my endeavours, have enabled me to have lived as well as any Woman of frugality and moderate desires ought to have wished. Upon the breaking out of the troubles, I came to a determination to share the fate of my Country and that I might not be merely a spectator, I made as hasty a close as I possibly could, of my commercial affairs, making it a point to collect and deposit in safe hands as much as would, whenever times and circumstances would permit, enable me to discharge my European debts which were indeed all I had, except about £—— put into my hands by Mr R. Senr in trust for my youngest Brother; but as a security for that I left and have yet a much larger sum in my Father's bonds. After I had happily collected & deposited the sum first mentioned, my outstanding debts began to be paid in depreciated money and as I never took the advantage of a single penny in that way I have sorely felt the pernicious effects of tenders Laws — I expect (and were I only to look forward to a provision for myself it would give me no uneasiness) to begin the World in a manner anew, with the consolation of having devoted the service of that time to my Country, which some others have spent in amassing fortunes upon its distresses. It has ever been a maxim with me to depend upon myself and not build upon the emoluments of Office which are as precarious as the events of life. They are well enough as contingencies and as Suit I have a right and reason to expect some advantages from them—Indeed some of my public Friends have been kind enough to assure me that a due recompense shall be made me for my adherence to the barren Military Line, where they flatter me with saying that I have been useful. Something handsome will devolve to me upon an event, which I shall esteem, should it please God to permit me to see, the most melancholy, next to one which I have already seen, of my life — This have as fully as the of a letter will admit made you acquainted with every thing relative to the transaction of which I have been speaking. It is with you to determine what shall be my future line of conduct. If I meet your disapprobation, I shall instantly relinquish all hopes of ever accomplishing a matter on which my happiness very much depends; for I too well know the high sense which my Cousin entertains of filial duty towards the tenderest and best of parents, to suppose that my influence would have any weight when opposed to his will. In such case I should severely feel my misfortune, but I beg you to be assured that it would in no degree lessen that respect and true regard which I have for you, and altho' necessity would require me to endeavour to cease to love the present object of my affections, I would never wish to forget how dear she had ever been to me. If on the contrary you should be good enough to permit me, circumstanced as I am, to prosecute my hopes, I shall most zealously set about making such arrangements as I trust will enable me, ere long, to support the most valuable of Women in a manner, tho far below her deserts, yet perhaps equal to her wishes — And here I cannot help repeating to you what she will do me the justice of saying I requested of her, that however favorable her sentiments might be of me at that time She would not look upon herself as debarred from, the liberty of accepting any other which might be made — In point of future she may have many far preferable to me but in warmth and sincerity of affection no man can go beyond me.

I shall probably have left Maryland before you can find it convenient to favor me with an answer — you will thereupon be pleased to commit your letter to the care of my Friend at Chester Town and they will forward it to me.

I am with the utmost Respect an
sincerest Esteem
D^r. Sir,
Y^{rs}

The Commission of Col. Tench Tilghman, from the original now in the possession of the family.

"THE UNITED STATES OF AMERICA IN CONGRESS ASSEM-
"BLED To Tench Tilghman, Esquire, GREETING. We,
" reposing especial trust and confidence in your Patriotism,
" Valour, Conduct and Fidelity, Do by these presents con-
" stitute and appoint you to be a LIEUTENANT COLONEL in
" the army of the United States, to rank as such from the
" first day of April 1777 ; you are therefore carefully and
" diligently to discharge the duty of a *Lieutenant Colonel*,
" by doing and performing all manner of things thereunto
" belonging. And we do strictly charge and require all
" Officers and Soldiers under your command, to be obe-
" dient to your orders as *Lieutenant Colonel*. And you are
" to observe and follow such orders and directions, from
" time to time, as you shall receive from this or a future
" Congress of the United States, or Committee of Con-
" gress for that purpose appointed, a Committee of the
" States, or Commander-in-chief for the time being of the
" Army of the United States, or any other, your superior
" Officer, according to the rules and discipline of war, in
" pursuance of the trust reposed in you. This commission
" to continue in force until revoked by this or a future
" Congress, the Committee of Congress, before mentioned,
" or a Committee of the States."

[United States of America Board of War]
" Witness his Excellency Samuel Hun-
" tington President of the Congress
" of the United States of America,
" at Philadelphia, the 30th day of
" May 1781 and in the fifth year
" of our Independence."

SAM^L. HUNTINGTON, *President.*

" Entered in the War Office and examined by
   " the Board attest Jos : Carleton
            Secretary of the Board of War."

Dear Sir,

The Convention of this State have appointed a committee of Correspondence for the Purpose of obtaining Intelligence from the army, of which Committee your acquaintance Mr R. R. Livingstone, and myself are members. They have empowered this Committee to employ a Gentleman near Head Quarters for communicating Intelligence to whom they have engaged to make an adequate compensation — Mr Livingstone and myself are anxious you should undertake this Task; in consequence of which I am requested to know your sentiments on this head — The Sum Ideal of your office will be to write a daily Letter which our Express will wait on you for — As you (I conceive)   head quarters a few short Notes of the Daily interesting   will serve as material for your — *Daily Advertiser.*

If your leisure will admit, and your willingness to oblige will make you overlook the little Éclat that attends this office, you will be pleased to commence your Correspondence by informing us of all such Public Incidents as you think interesting —

The Letters you write will be of a Public Nature, as the Committee are obliged to lay them before the Convention.

I am Sir — with great personal Regards

Your Obed^t. H^{ble}. Servt.

W^m. Duer.

War Office 2nd December 1785

Dear Sir

I have to acknowledge the receipt of your favor of the 21st ultimo

The board of treasury at my instance will remit you immediately an order for the sum of four hundred dollars on their Agent in Maryland

I will thank you to inform me of the receipt of the sum that I may have the pleasure of writing you an official letter on the occasion

I expect in the course of a month or two to receive all the swords which were voted by Congress as testimonies of their special approbation; upon receiving them I shall have the pleasure of transmitting yours

     I am
      Dear Sir
       With great sincerity
        Your affectionate
         Humble Servant
          H. Knox

Col°
 Tench Tilghman

     War Office 7 December, 1785.

Dear Sir

I now enclose you the order of the board of treasury on Thomas Harwood Esqr. commissioner of the continental loan office State of Maryland for the sum of four hundred dollars to pay for the horse ordered to be presented to you by the resolve of Congress of the 29th of October 1785.

I will thank you to enclose to me by the return of post a receipt for this order which must serve as my voucher at the Comptrollers office for the disbursement of the money which is charged to me by the treasury board: you will please to specify the purpose for which you receive the money.

     I am Dear Sir
      Your very humble servant
        H. Knox

Tench Tilghman Esqr.

War Office of the United States
New York May 30th. 1786

Madam

I have the honor to enclose for your satisfaction, a copy of a resolve of Congress of the 29th of October 1781.

During the last year, I had the honor of presenting to Colonel Tilghman, the horse agreeably to the direction of the resolve, and I then mentioned to him, that I should forward the sword, as soon as it should be finished.

But death, the inevitable tribute of our system, has prematurely deprived you of the most tender and virtuous companion, and the United States, of an able and upright patriot. While you are overwhelmed with affliction, your friends unavailingly condole with you on an event, which they could not prevent, and to which they also must submit.

When time shall have smoothed the severities of your grief, you will derive consolation from the reflection that Colonel Tilghman acted well, his part on the theatre of human life, and that the supreme authority of the United States, have expressly given their sanction to his merit.

The sword directed to be presented to him, which I have the honor to transmit to you, will be an honorable and perpetual evidence of his merit and of the applause of his country.

I have the honor to be Madam,
With perfect respect,
Your most obedient and
Very humble Servant
H. KNOX

New York, 13 Augt. 1776.

Hon^d. Sir

Since I wrote to you last, 96 Sail of Vessels have arrived at the watering place and within the Hook, part of them this day. We suppose they are the Transports with Foreign Troops.— To our great Amazement they still con-

tinue inactive, which is much in our fav^r. for we are receiving Reinforcements every day. The Pennsylvania and Maryland Troops are a prodigious thing for us — Even the Eastern people acknowledge their Superiority — The General has brigaded them together and puts the utmost Confidence in them. Our Strength by Land is very great, besides our Musquetry and Rifles behind Lines, Col^o. Knox, the Commandant of Artillery, tells me he has a train of 40 Field pieces ready at a Moments Warning. This is not merely Report of the Colonels, but I have seen the Guns with all the Artillery Stores ready for action. You can have no Idea of the Generals Merit and Abilities without being with him, few Words serve him, but they are to the purpose, and an Order once given by him is implicity obeyed thro' every Department. His civilities to me have been more than I had a right to expect, but I endeavour to make it up by my Assiduity in executing his Commands, in some of which I have given him very particular Satisfaction. I have still the Happiness to be
Y^{rs}. most dutifully and affect^y
Tench Tilghman.

New York, 15 Augt. 1776.

Hon^d. Sir

I have yours of the 11th Ins^t. which mentions your having wrote one before, but it never came to my hands, be pleased to say in your next whether you sent it ppost or by a private opportunity. If the latter I will endeavour to trace it. You see from this Miscarriage that nothing but of a public nature should at this time be trusted to Paper. I can assure you your Anxiety on my Account is groundless on the Score of Expence, Company & Habit of Idleness. As to the first I live at less in proportion than at Philad. the second my acquaintance is confined to two or three young Gentlemen of the Generals Family, and to the last you cannot conceive what a constant Scene of Business we are engaged in. My Intent is not to stay with the Army longer than the active part of the Campaign as I had taken a military part, I could not in honour withdraw or hold myself back, when I found that contrary to all Faith and Expectation the Olive Branch was presented accompanied with Terms the most ignominious. When you say "bear with me this once and I will say no more on the Subject," you seem to hint as if you thought, that your Advice would be disagreeable or set hard upon me, but indeed you are mistaken, I know it proceeds from your Regard to me and from no other motive. We are told that the whole of General Howe's Forces are now arrived, and from the movement of yesterday we expected an Attack this morning, but it has rained very hard all Night and that perhaps has hindered them — One of the Letters you inclosed me was from Mr. Wm. Brown of Annapolis respecting a Note of Hand of Carpenter Whartons, go let Billy write to him and inform him that nothing has been rec^d since the £40 he paid to Lendrum — My love to my Sisters. I am most dutifully and Affecty yrs

TENCH TILGHMAN.

New York 18th Augt. 1776.

Hon Sir

I have two of your Letters before me. One of them enclosed a Letter from Mr Chew to E. Tilghman who is now here. He is well provided for, as Assistant Brigade Major to Lord Stirling's Brigade, which is composed intirely of the Maryland and pennsylvania Forces. The Phoenix and the Rose Men of War came down the River this morning which occasioned a smart Cannonade between them and our Batteries, but as they had a smart Breeze and the Tide in their fav^r they got quickly by without receiving or doing any damage. Our Fire Ships got on Board of them a few Nights ago, the Phoenix with difficulty cleared herself, but her Tender was burnt. I fancy the fear of being attacked again in that way brought them down to join the Fleet in the Bay. The Chevaux de-frise to compleat the Obstruction of the Channel at Fort Washington had not got up owing to head winds, otherwise these Ships would have found the greatest difficulty in getting down again. A flag came off yesterday from the Fleet, the General sent me to receive it. I found Lord Drummond in the Boat, who delivered me a Letter for Genl. Washington it contained a plan of his own for an Accommodation, and wanted to come on shore and go to Philad^a to propose it to Congress. He says it has my Lord Howes Approbation, But not a syllable from my Lord himself. This is certainly strange trifling Conduct. What right has any private Man to propose terms when he does not pretend to have any power or Authority to do it. However the General has sent the Plan to Congress and waits their Direction. But he would not suffer my Lord to come on Shore. I take your Caution to me in Regard to my Health very kindly, but I assure you, you need be under no Apprehension of my losing it on the Score of Excess in living, that Vice is banished from this Army and the Generals Family in particular. We never sup, but go early to bed and are early up. The New England Troops are the only sick ones, and a good deal of that is Laziness. I have not yet seen young Mr. Williams but I will find him out and take notice of him. The Fleet and Army remain intirely inactive. I don't believe they want to fight. If they do they have missed their time. We are very well provided for them now, but a few Weeks ago were very much the reverse.

    I am with the warmest affection,
       Y^r most dutiful Son
         TENCH TILGHMAN.

Your missing Letter has come to hand

(Envelope addressed to James Tilghman Esq. Philadelphia.)

New York, 19 Augt. 1776.

Hon^d Sir

I have already wrote you by this post, but since I closed my Letter yours came to hand. There will be no difficulty in sending an open Letter to my Brother by the first Flag that goes off — By a Deserter from the Roe Buck last night we hear that she has a malignant Fever on board and is riding quarantine. The Hessians are also sickly the Deserter says they have the yellow fever. We can plainly see their Encampment intirely separate from the other Troops. I am certain something must be the Matter or they would have attacked.

Reinforcements from N England are coming in very fast—

I am most dutifully Yrs.
TENCH TILGHMAN.

Head Quarters N York 3rd Sepr. 1776.

Hon^d. Sir

I have attempted to write to you several times since our Return from Long Island, but have been as often interrupted by the vast hurry of Business in which the General is engaged. He is obliged to see into, and in a Manner fill every Department, which is too much for one Man — Our Retreat before an Enemy much superior in Numbers, over a wide River, and not very well furnished with Boats certainly does Credit to our Generals. The thing was conducted with so much Secrecy that neither subalterns or privates knew that the whole Army was to cross back again to N York, they thought only a few Regiments were to go back. General Howe has not yet landed upon this Island, but I imagine something of that kind is in Agitation, as the Fleet draw nearer and nearer, they are now about long Cannon Shot from the Battery, but no firing on either Side. We shall be prepared to meet them here or retreat over Kings Bridge as we shall find Occasion, our supernumerary and heavy Stores are removed, we must leave our heavy Cannon behind us in Case of Retreat, but I dont know that that will be any loss, as we never used them to much Advantage. By Returns made this day from the Northern Army, Gates is getting it into fine Order, they have ten thousand effective Men and a very considerable force afloat upon the Lake. Burgoyne has no Chance of making an Irruption this Campaign. The Behaviour of the Southern Troops in the late Action has shamed the Northern People, they confess themselves unequal to them in Officers and Discipline. No Regular Troops ever made a more gallant Resistance than Smallwood's Regiment. If the others had behaved as well, if Genl. Howe had obtained a Victory at all it would have been dearly bought — I hope we shall yet come off with a saving Game —

    I am most dutifully & Affect^y Yrs.

        TENCH TILGHMAN.

     New.York 9th. Sepr. 1776—

Hond Sir

All Matters have remained quiet since I wrote you last, except that two Batteries of 3 Guns each were opened yesterday ag^t our Battery at Hell Gate. They threw a Number of Shot and Shells into our Fort, but only killed one man and wounded two slightly. The General sent me up last Night to see what Situation things were in, when I found our Fortification but little damaged, not more than could be repaired in an hour. One of their Batteries had been silent for some Hours, and what shot they threw while I was there went far over our Works. We last night sent up some heavier Cannon with which they have been pretty warmly at work this morning, but the firing has in a great Measure ceased again — We are now in such a Situation, that we can effect a very hasty Retreat from hence if necessary, all our heavy Stores and Incumbrances being removed to Kings bridge and up the River. We have good men at Kings Bridge preparing fortifyed posts, that we may not be uncovered if a Retreat should be determined on. You may remember that you once mentioned, that the Destruction of New York was left to the General, so far from it, that he wrote to Congress for an explicit Answer on that head, and they have directed him by a Resolve to preserve the City at all Events, that is, if he was obliged to abandon not to suffer the Soldiery to do any damage. I never saw any Man so strictly observant of the preservation of private property, he never fails to punish any Breach that comes under his Observation: But I am sorry to say that most of his Officers do not keep up the same Discipline. I sent my Brothers Letter by a Flag. I am in great hopes that this Campaign will insensibly waste away without much Bloodshed, I know the General is determined to avoid a Battle for more Reasons than one. My best love to my sisters and all the Family my good Grandmother in particular.

I am most dutifully & affec^{ty}. Y^{rs}.

TENCH TILGHMAN.

P. S. As the post office is removed from hence all our Letters go by Express to Philad^a. If you or any of my Friends write to me and will give the Letters to Mr. Morris he will send them by Return of the Expresses.

10th: Your Letters of the 28th: Augt. 2^d & 6th. Sepr. have just come to hand they have been laying at Dob's ferry 24 Miles from hence, to which place the post office is removed. Doc^r Franklins Invitation to my Lord Howe, to meet him and the other Commissioners at Amboy or Staten Island as might be most agreable to his Lordship went on board yesterday Evening. His Lordship has not returned an Answer as he had to consult his Brother the

Gen¹. I wish our Gen¹ could have been of the party. Lord Howe returned an Answer to Doc^r. Franklin this Afternoon, which is sent to the Doc^r. who is to be at Amboy tomorrow. But whether his Lordship accedes to the Meeting we dont know.

Head Quarters, Harlem Heights, Monday,
Hon^d Sir   16 Sepr. 1776.

Our Army totally evacuated New York yesterday, the Enemy landed a party of about 3000 from Appearance four miles above the City where they encamped last Night. They kept up a very heavy fire from their Ships while their Men were landing, altho' no Body opposed them, I imagine they did it, thinking we might have men concealed behind some lines on the Water side. We removed every thing that was valuable, some heavy Cannon excepted, before we left the Town. Our army is posted as advantageously as possible for Security, out of reach of the Fire of the Ships from either River and upon high Grounds of difficult Access. I dont know whether the New Eng^d. Troops will stand there, but I am sure they will not upon open Ground. I had a Specimen of that yesterday. Hear two Brigades ran away from a small advanced party of the Regulars, tho' the General did all in his power to convince them they were in no danger. He laid his Cane over many of the Officers who shewed their men the Example of running. These were militia, the New England continental Troops are much better. The post is now so irregular and our Quarters so subject to be shifted that you will be pleased to put any Letters for me into M^r. Morris's Hands or some Gentleman of the Congress and get them forwarded with the General's. He must alway be found wherever he may be. We are just going out to put Matters in the best Situation for defence. I have only time to say

I am truly Y^{rs} most dutifully & affect^y
TENCH TILGHMAN.

P.S. Be pleased to get Ned Tilghman to inform Mrs. Duncan and Mr. John Taylor that I rec^d the money sent for their Friends who are prisoners, and that it shall be sent by a Flag that goes to exchange Genl. Sullivan & L^d. Stirling for Genl. Prescot and McDonald.

Head Quarters Col^o. Morris's 19th Sepr. 1776.

Hon^d. Sir

I wrote you a few Lines since we removed to this place. On Monday last we had a pretty sharp Skirmish with the British Troops which was brought on in the following Manner. The General rode down to our farthest Lines, and when he came near them heard a firing which he was informed was between our Scouts and the out Guards of the Enemy. When our men came in they informed the General that there were a party of about 300 behind a woody hill, tho' they only showed a very small party to us. Upon this General laid a plan for attacking them in the Rear and cutting off their Retreat which was to be effected in the following Manner. Major Leitch with three companies of Col^o. Weedons Virginia Regiment, and Col^o. Knowlton with his Rangers were to steal round while a party were to march towards them and seem as if they intended to attack in front, but not to make any real Attack till they saw our Men fairly in their Rear. The Bait took as to one part, as soon as they saw our party in front the Enemy ran down the Hill and took possession of some Fences and Bushes and began to fire at them, but at too great distance to do much execution: Unluckily Col^o. Knowlton and Major Leitch began their Attack too soon, it was rather in Flank than in Rear. The Action now grew warm, Major Leitch was wounded early in the Engagement and Col^o. Knowlton soon after, the latter mortally, he was one of the bravest and best officers in the Army. Their Men notwithstanding persisted with the greatest Bravery.

The Gen¹. finding they wanted support ordered over part of Col°. Griffiths's and part of Col°. Richardson's Maryland Regiments, these Troops tho' young charged with as much Bravery as I can conceive, they gave two fires and then rushed right forward which drove the Enemy from the Wood into a Buckwheat field, from whence they retreated. The General fearing (as we afterwards found) that a large Body was coming up to support them, sent me over to bring our Men off. They gave a Hurra and left the Field in good Order. We had about 40 wounded and a very few killed. A Serjeant who deserted says their Accounts were 89 wounded and 8 killed, but in the latter he is mistaken for we have buried more than double that Number — We find their force was much more considerable than we imagined when the General ordered the Attack. It consisted of the 2ᵈ. Battⁿ. of light Infantry, a Battⁿ. of the Royal Highlanders and 3 Compˢ. of Hessian Rifle Men. The prisoners we took, told us, they expected our Men would have run away as they did the day before, but that they were never more surprised than to see us advancing to attack them. The Virginia and Maryland Troops bear the Palm. They are well officered and behave with as much regularity as possible, while the Eastern people are plundering everything that comes in their way. An Ensign is to be tried for marauding to-day, the Gen¹. will execute him if he can get a Court martial to convict him — I like our post here exceedingly, I think if we give it up it is our own faults. You must excuse me to my other friends for not writing to them. I can hardly find time to give you a Line —

I am most dutifully & affecʸ Yʳˢ.

TENCH TILGHMAN.

Head Quarters Harlem Heights, 25ᵗʰ Sepʳ. 1776.
Honᵈ Sir

I take the opportunity of letting you know by Mʳ.

Bache, who has been here establishing the post office, that all Matters between the two armies have remained perfectly quiet since the 16th May and various will be the Reports concerning the setting fire to New York, if it was done designedly, it was without the knowledge or Approbation of any commanding officer in this Army, and indeed so much time had elapsed between our quitting the City and the fire, that it can never be fairly attributed to the Army. Indeed every man belonging to the Army who remained in or were found near the City were made close prisoners. Many Acts of barbarous cruelty were committed upon poor creatures who were perhaps flying from the flames, the Soldiers and Sailors looked upon all who were not in the military line as guilty, and burnt and cut to pieces many. But this I am sure was not by Order. Some were executed next day upon good Grounds. The greatest part of Broad Street and Broad Way as far up as the old City Hall is burnt. Kennedy's House and the next to it escaped as did Hulls Tavern. Trinity Church is also burnt. I went down to the Enemy's lines yesterday with a Flag to settle the Exchange of prisoners, which I believe will generally take place. I met a very civil Gentleman with whom I had an Hours conversation while my Dispatches were going up to Genl Howe. He told me that every vigorous Step was taken to keep the British Army under the strictest Discipline, but that the Hessians could not be restrained without breaking with them as they claimed a right of plunder, and that Genl Howe was obliged to pay for the Excesses they committed. As Mr. Bache has fixed an Office near Head Quarters and which is always to move with the General you may send Letters for me by the post as usual. My best love to all at home.

I am your dutiful and affec^t Son
TENCH TILGHMAN.

Head Quarters Harlem Heights 3 Octob., 1776.
Hon⁴. Sir

We have all Hands been so busily employed for some time past, that I have not had time to acknowledge the Rec‍ᵗ. of your two last letters — I was surprised with the sight of Mr. James Allen two days ago. Curiosity brought him here to see the Situation of Things, he informed me that you was going to Maryland, I therefore have directed this letter to be opened in your Absence, that my Sisters may know I am well. Sam Earle is incamped close to Head Quarters, so that I can see him often without any Inconvenience, he is highly spoken of by his commanding officers, as an officer of uncommon merit and Attention for his years. Gen‍ˡ. Howe has made no one Move like an intended Attack, he like us is attending to his own Defence, he has thrown up Lines along his whole front from the East to the North River. There is one circumstance lately turned up which corroborates an opinion that I have long held, which is, that Gen‍ˡ. Howe never had so strong an Army as was given out. The circumstance is this. One of our Cruisers to the Eastward has taken a Transport, one of six Sail, bound from New York to the West Indies to bring the Garrisons from thence. We know that the Garrisons there were very much reduced before, and from the late favourable Disposition shown by the French Governor to Cap‍ᵗ. Weeks, I should think our Garrisons in the Islands ought rather to be increased than diminished. Gen‍ˡ. Sullivan is positive that in the present Situation of their affairs they cannot bring above 12000 Men to act against our Main Body, he makes the following Estimate. Their whole 20000 effective Men which I dare say is sufficient for the Casualties in a large Army are immense. 3000 Men are destined for the Garrison of New York. 1900 are upon Staten Island. About 1200 up and down upon Long Island, as many upon Bergen and there is a considerable Number upon Montresors & Buchanans Islands. If so Sullivan is right, and this corresponds with the Intelligence we have recd. from others. Yesterday Morning we had Occasion to bring off a parcel of Hay and Grain from Harlem, to effect this with Safety, a covering party of 1000 Men were ordered under Arms. As the Enemy could plainly discover our Men marching towards their right Flank, I believe they imagined an attack was intended upon their Lines, they immediately beat to arms, struck their Tents and manned their Lines. Upon perceiving our real Intentions they let us alone, set down again and let us bring off the Grain. I really think Matters look like a bloodless Campaign. I mean as to anything general ——

    I am your most dutiful & Affect. Son
        TENCH TILGHMAN.

    Head Quarters Harlem Heights 7th. Octob 1776.
Hon{d}. Sir

I yesterday recd. two Letters of the 27th and 28th. Sepr. it makes me exceedingly unhappy to think that my Situation, which is not more dangerous than that of any other Man in this Army, should make you and my Sisters so uneasy. I know it proceeds from your Affection for me and therefore I feel it more sensibly. I am detained here by no particular Engagements entered into with the General, so far from it, that tho' he has repeatedly told me I ought to have a Compensation for my Services, I have refused, telling him, that as I only intended to stay with him as long as the active part of the Campaign lasted, I wished to serve as a Volunteer. If I had no other Tie than that of Honour I could not leave the Army just now, but there is another if possible more binding with me. The General has treated in a Manner the most confidential, he has intrusted me and one other Gentleman of his

Family, his Secretary, with his most private Opinions on more Occasions than one, and I am sure they have been given in a different Manner than they would have been to some others that the World imagines have great Influence over him. Was I to leave him now, crowded as he is by Business, of good part of which I am able to relieve him, would not my conduct appear suspicious to him, would it not look as if I had ingratiated myself with him purposely to make myself Master of his Secrets, and then to take an Advantage. The season will soon arrive when every Man not in any particular Command may leave the Army with Credit, and till that I cannot think of returning home. With respect to what you mention of Mr. Morris's wanting our Books to ascertain the Amount of any Debt, he should by all Means have them, there are no Secrets in them. The Bond of Gibbs to Phil Francis is in my Iron Chest among some papers tied up and indorsed "belonging to P. F"—We shall see this Winter how Matters are like to settle, if I live, I can then determine what is to be done in the Way of Business. I would chuse to hold fast what I have got till things are upon a more certain Foundation than they are at present or have been for some time.

The two Armies are as quiet as if they were a Thousand Miles apart, it begins to look very like an inactive Campaign. Nothing will make me so happy as to hear that your fears on my Account are more composed, I have wrote to my Sisters endeavouring to pacify theirs.

I am y^r. most dutiful & affec^t. Son
TENCH TILGHMAN.

Head Quarters Harlem Heights 13th Octob, 1776.
Hon^d. Sir

I have just time to acknowledge the Rect. of your two Letters. All our attention is taken up in watching the

Motions of the Enemy who moved a considerable part of their Army up the Sound yesterday and landed them at a place called Frogs point. By their not moving from thence it looks as if they wanted to divert our Attention while some other Object is in view. By Letters last Night from Boston we have the following Acct. taken from a London print of the 28th Augt. "the Spaniards had invaded Portugal which has thrown the Ministry and Nation into the greatest Consternation. A Vessel is taken from London with a Cargo of £37000 stirling on Board and not a day passes but a Victualler, State Ship or some other prize is carried in —

    I am in Haste
      Y^{rs} most dutifully & affect^{ly}
        TENCH TILGHMAN.

    Valentines Hill 4 Miles from Kingsbridge
       22^d October 1776.

Hon^d Sir

We have been so much upon the move since Genl. Howe bent his Course up the Sound, that I have not had time to set down to write you a Line. The Enemy hug the Shore and we keep close upon their left Flank which prevents their turning over towards the North River which is evidently their Design, we still keep our old post at Harlem. Yesterday Morning Major Rogers advanced with his Regiment of Rangers to a little Town called Maroneck where we had had some Stores, but they were removed. The Militia posted there, ran away as usual, which put Rogers in a State of perfect Security. The General judging the thing would be so, detached Major Green with 150 Men from the 1st & 3^d Virginia Regiments and Col^l Haslet with 600 from his own and other Regiments to fall upon Rogers in the Night, which they did and put him and his Party intirely to the Rout, and had not the Guides posted Haslet wrong the whole party consisting of 400 must have fallen into our Hands. As it was, they brought in 36 prisoners, 60 Arms and a good many Blankets, they counted 25 killed in one Orchard, how many got off wounded we dont know. As they were near their main Body it would not do to pursue. We have 12 Men wounded among them Maj^r Green in the Shoulder and Capt. Pope slightly. We are just setting off for the White Plains where the General intends to fix Head Quarters for the present.

I am y^{rs} most dutifully & affect^{ly}
TENCH TILGHMAN.

White Plains 31st October 1776.

Hon^d. Sir

As all Accounts of Actions are much exaggerated before they reach you, I always take the earliest Opportunity of informing you of the Truth and at the same time of letting you know that I am safe and well. On Monday morning we rec^d. Information that the Enemy were in Motion and in march towards our Lines, all our Men were immediately at their Alarm Posts and about 2000 detached to give the Enemy as much annoyance as possible on their Approach. There were likewise a few Regiments posted upon a Hill on our Right, of which we had not had time to throw up Works, which Hill commanded our Lines which were but slight and temporary ones. About Noon the Enemy appeared full in our Front in vast Numbers, their Light Horse reconnoitered our Lines, and I suppose not chusing to attack them, filed off towards the Hill, on which they began a most furious Cannonade, followed by a heavy Column of Infantry, our Troops made as good a Stand as could be expected and did not quit the Ground, till they came to push their Bayonets. We lost about 100 killed and wounded. Smallwoods Regiment suffered most, he himself is wounded in the Hand and Hip but not badly. Capt. Braco and Scott killed. From all Accounts of Deserters and prisoners the English Army suffered more than we did, for as their Body was large, the Shot from our Field pieces and Musquets, could scarcely miss doing damage. Six of their Light Horse Men were killed and one of the Horses, a very fine one, taken by one of Miles's Officers and made a present to the General — Content with the possession of the Hill, they sat down about Six hundred yards from us and have never fired a Gun since. We have moved all our Tents and Baggage and Stores before their Faces, and have put them on the Heights just above the plain where they at first were. Every Motion of Genl. Howe since he first landed has evidently been to get in the Rear of this Army, and destroy them by cutting off their Communication for Supplies from the Country. To do this will be extremely difficult if not impracticable, all the Ground he has gained from the Sound Westward, is but about Six Miles and that thro' an open Country where we never thought of attacking them on Account of their great Train of Artillery. They have now just reached the Hills, which are very high and broken, and of Consequence their Motion must be very slow, as we have taken all the Passes. Their heavy Horse from England are all ruined on the passage, we took a Commissary last Night who informs us that 900 Horse were embarked, they were on Board 26 weeks, 500 died on the Passage and 400 were landed yesterday reduced to Skeletons. This is a monstrous Disappointment to them — Much has been said of the Clemency of the British Army, at first landing they attempted to restrain the Soldiery, at least from hurting what were deemed Tories, but the Hessians would not be restrained, they made no Distinction and Genl. Howe dare not punish them. The British Troops seeing the Foreigners rioting in plenty and plundering all before them, grew restless and uneasy, and are now indulged in the same Excesses. The people who, tho' informed against as Tories, were protected by Genl. Washington and paid for what they would sell, have come in and informed us that they were stripped of their all whenever the Enemy advanced upon them. The Foreigners who have been taken, all agree that a Liberty of plunder without Distinction is what they expect and insist upon. New York was set on fire by a Party of them who robbed a Rum Store and set the Fire agoing in their Liquor. After this, which is strictly true, can they ask the Americans to lay down their Arms, before such a licentious Crew are removed? We are on Horseback or busy from Sun Rise to Sun Set, and all the time I find to write is at Night. I met with an Accident at Harlem Heights which I look upon as irreparable, I mean the loss of my faithful saddle Horse, who died in a few Hours, from every Appearance in high Order and Spirit. I had rode him gently most of the day and never observed him fail, but about two Miles from Head Quarters. I suppose it must have been Bots. I have mounted myself upon a pretty Mare, that will make an excellent Breeder, if I get her safe home. My best love to my Grandmother and Sisters and all my Friends, I would write oftener to them and to you, but as I said before I have not time.

    I am with the greatest affection
          Y^r. most dutiful son
             Tench Tilghman.

  (Envelope addressed to
    James Tilghman Esq.
     Philadelphia.)

Head Quarters near Coryels Ferry, 16th Decem^r 1776.
Hon^d. Sir.

A Gentleman from philad^a some days ago informed me that you were gone to Maryland with my Sisters, but Gen Sinclair who is just come up, tells me you are still in Town.

The Motions of the Enemy for a day or two past looks like going into Winter Quarters, and the Accounts brought in by prisoners confirm it — A Captain Murray who was prisoner at New York, and came out by Exchange yesterday, told Col° Cadwallader that he saw Andrew, John and William Allen at Trenton, M°Pherson who by some means got over the River to Trenton, told Gen¹ Washington that he had seen Andr^w Allen there, but this we did not believe till the Account seemed confirmed by Capt Murray. If this should not be true, the Gentlemen should contradict it as early and publicly as possible, otherwise mischief may ensue, for people will perhaps insist that they have been over to make their peace in a private way — Lee was picked up a few days ago in a strange Manner for so old a Soldier, he knew he was in a Country full of concealed Enemies, and still trusted himself three miles from his Army with only a Guard of a dozen Men — I despair of seeing Philad^a till the General goes there himself, Business seems to multiply upon him as the Campaign draws to an end, indeed the Weight of the whole War may justly be said to lay upon his Shoulders — I just snatch a time while others are at Dinner to say

      I am y^r. dutiful & Affec^t Son
          TENCH TILGHMAN.

(Envelope Addressed to
James Tilghman Esq.
Philadelphia.)

    Head Quarters, Newtown 27th. Decem^r. 1776.
Hon^d. Sir

I have the pleasure to inform you that I am safe and well after a most successful Enterprise against three Regiments of Hessians consisting of about 1500 Men lying in Trenton, which was planned and executed under his Excellencys immediate command. Our party amounted to 2400 Men, we crossed the River at M°Konkeys Ferry 9 Miles above Trenton, the Night was excessively severe, both cold and snowey, which the Men bore without the least murmur. We were so much delayed in crossing the River, that we did not reach Trenton till eight OClock, when the division which the General headed in person, attacked the Enemy's out post. The other Division which marched the lower Road, attacked the advanced post at Phil. Dickinsons, within a few minutes after we began ours. Both parties pushed on with so much rapidity, that the Enemy had scarce time to form, our people advanced up to the Mouths of their Field pieces, shot down their Horses and brought off the Cannon. About 600 run off upon the Bordentown Road the moment the Attack began, the remainder finding themselves surrounded laid down their Arms. We have taken 30 Officers and 886 privates among the former Col°. Rahls the Commandant who is wounded. The General left him and the other wounded Officers upon their parole, under their own Surgeons, and gave all the privates, their Baggage. Our Loss is only Capt. Washington and his Lieutenant slightly wounded and two privates killed and two wounded. If the Ice had not prevented Genl. Ewing from crossing at Trenton Ferry, and Col° Cadwalader from doing the same at Bristol, we should have followed the Blow and drove every post below Trenton. The Hessians have laid all waste since the British Troops went away, the Inhabitants had all left the Town and their Houses were stripped and torn to pieces. The Inhabitants about the Country told us, that the British protections would not pass among the Hessians. I am informed that many people have of choice kept their Effects in Philad^a. supposing if Genl. Howe got possession that they would be safe, so they may be, if he only carries British Troops with him, but you may depend it is not in his power, neither does he pretend to restrain the Foreigners. I have just snatched time to scrawl these few lines by Col°. Baylor, who is going to Congress —

    I am your most dutiful and Affect. Son
          TENCH TILGHMAN.

Head Quarters Newtown 29 Decem^r 1776

Dear and Hon^d. Sir

Yours is this moment put into my Hands but you would receive mine by Col°. Baylor giving you a full Account of the Affair at Trenton a little after you dispatched the Messenger — We are just going over to Jersey again in pursuit of the Remainder of the Hessian Army who have left Bordentown — The General waits while I write this much. My most affect. love to my Sisters.

I am y^r most dutiful Son
TENCH TILGHMAN.

Head Quarters Morris Town 11th Jany. 1777.

Hon^d. Sir.

It generally happens that when an opportunity to Philad^a offers, my time is taken up with the public dispatches. Since our lucky Stroke upon the Enemy's rear at princetown, they have evacuated all their posts in Jersey except Amboy and Brunswic, where they are pent up almost destitute of Provision, Fuil and Forage. Depending upon the whole province of Jersey for supplies this winter, they had established no general Magazine, but ordered small ones to be laid up in and about the several Towns; all these have fallen into our hands. We found most of the Mills on Raritan full of Flour, laid up for the British Commissaries. There is no good Blood between the English and Foreigners, the former tax the latter with Negligence in the loss of Trenton, which they say is the cause of their Misfortunes. I rec^d a parcel of hard money from you for Hackets Son, but as most of the prisoners taken at Fort Washington are sent out, I think it likely that Hacket may be among them, if so, sending in the money would probably be to lose it. I will therefore keep it till I hear more of the Matter. Whenever you write to or see my Sisters remember me most affect^y. to them.

I am most dutifully and Affect^y. Y^{rs}
TENCH TILGHMAN.

CORRESPONDENCE. 151

Head Quarters Morristown 22^d. Feby. 1777

Hon^d Sir

I yesterday had the pleasure of receiving yours of the 10th with one from my Sister inclosed. I do not write to you so regularly as I otherwise would, because you are often absent from Philad^a. and my letters would probably miscarry for want of being regularly forwarded from thence. I will in future put them under cover to M^r. Morris, who will deliver them to you if you are in town and if you are in Maryland send them carefully to you. Send any for me to him and he will forward them with the Generals packets. I wish you had mentioned what my Brother James's Views are in going to the West Indies, I imagine it must be to the Foreign Islands, if so, perhaps I might procure him Credentials that would be very serviceable to him. I think with you that the prospect of peace is not very near at hand, but I am of the opinion that I ever entertained, that its owing to a want of Unanimity in the people. After the two successful Blows at Trenton & princetown, had the Army which we had with us at the latter only remained entire, I am confident, that Genl. Howes army could not have remained in Jersey. But ours were mostly Militia and the Fatigue that they had undergone made them anxious to get home. If the whole of the last Campaign when the British Army was in its Zenith, was spent in a fruitless endeavour to bring ours to engagement, which they once had a fair opportunity of at the White plains, what are they to do the ensuing Campaign, when their Army is reduced by killed, wounded, prisoners, deserters and the common Casualties from twenty odd thousand to Sixteen thousand which is their utmost extent. For as Deserters from every Corps in their Army have fallen into our hands and every now and then orderly Books and Returns, we can from all these form a very good Estimate of their Numbers. One capital Loss they have met which is an irreparable one, their Horses, which are reduced to the lowest Ebb, and must in all probability perish before next Grass. Gen¹. Dickinson took upwards of an hundred of them six Weeks ago and they were then almost upon the lift as we call it. I know you are of opinion that the accounts of the plundering of the British and Hessian Army is exaggerated, but indeed it is not only confirmed by the people of the Country, but by the British Officers who we have taken, who confess it freely. I will give you a proof of what was intended had Philadelphia fallen into their Hands, and which I have from an intercepted Letter that fell into my Hands in a most wonderful way. When the British Army lay at Trenton an Officer of ours went in with a Flag. A letter was given to him unsealed for a Gentleman in Philadᵃ. The General desired me to inspect it. I thought I knew the hand, but the Name I did not, the Style was mysterious and unintelligible except to those in the Secret. This raised all our Suspicions and we were determined to unravel it. Chancing to hold the letter near the fire, new Characters began to appear, and we soon discovered that the whole Sheet was fully written with some composition that appeared when warmed. It was from a Gentleman nearly connected with our family and gave an account to his Friends of the intentions of the Enemy. The River was to be crossed upon the Ice and the Army marched directly to Philadᵃ. when every house, which the owners had left, was to be given up to be plundered, and the Gentleman pressed all his Friends and Acquaintance to remove in. I own I was shocked at the thoughts of what would be the Consesequence were they to get into the Town. Soldiery once let loose are not easily restrained, and as they would probably have found the Houses empty of People, empty of Goods, rather than have been disappointed of their prey, they would have fallen on without Distinction. Who is safe while an Army kept for such purposes remains in a Country. From the Moment I saw the first proclamation, I was convinced, no terms were to be expected but blind Submission, and from that Moment I was determined never to submit to them. I wish the Situation of Affairs would permit me to leave the General for a little time, the Weight of his Business falls upon M^r. Harrison and myself, but as he (M^r. Harrison is often troubled with a most painful disorder, the piles) I then work double tides. My Absence is doubtless some detriment to my private Affairs but not much. Debts in the hands of good people are paid in. There are Securities for others and those that are unwilling to pay could not be compelled were I at home. I have the happiness and satisfaction of feeling that I have contributed largely by my personal application to the Cause in which I am engaged and which I am certain will end in the Freedom of this Country which I hope to see a happy and settled one. If it pleases God to spare the life of the honestest Man that I believe ever adorned human Nature I have no doubt of it. I think I know the Sentiments of his heart and in prosperity and Adversity I never knew him utter a Wish or drop an expression that did not tend to the good of his Country regardless of his own Interest. He is blessed wherever he goes for the Tory is protected in person and property equally with the Whig. And indeed I often think more, for it is his Maxim to convert by good Usage and not by Severity. If we succeed I am in no fear of making myself ample amends for my lost time. If we fail, anything in this Country is not worth a thought. I know we do not agree in political Sentiments quite, but that I am convinced does not in the least abate that ardent Affection which I have for you and which makes me happy far happier than any other title when I call myself

     Y^r most dutiful Son
       TENCH TILGHMAN.

P.S. pray let me know whether Ned Shippen got safe home, I procured his Release that day our Armies engaged at Trenton. I do not think the M^r A—s used him kindly, if they carried him with them from home, they should not have left him at his time of life at Trenton.

Head Quarters Morris Town 17th March 1777.
Hon^d Sir

I had, a few days ago, the pleasure of yours of the 28th last month. My Brother James only tells me he is going to the West Indies, but does not say where or upon what prospects. M^r. Morris writes that the Ships of War have left Chesapeak, if so, he may get out if he is ready. The concealed Letter which I mentioned in my last, was never sent to any public Body, the Substance only was. I cannot forget or be mistaken in that part which relates to plundering of all Houses where the Inhabitants should not be found in them, and the Gentleman particularly desires that one or two of his Friends may remove back to Town, and that a guard may be set over his Store and information given to whom it belonged to save the Effects that were in it. You say supposing Genl How has but Sixteen thousand Men, can you look such a Force in the face? I answer yes, when the new Army draws together, which will be much more respectable than has ever been in the field yet, because, they will be men enlisted for a length of time and therefore free from all these whims and caprices which ever attend Troops, who are scarcely collected before they disband again. There has likewise been a prodigious reform among the Officers — But you must remember that if Genl. Howe takes the Field, he cannot carry anything near that Number of Troops with him, without abandoning all the Conquests of last Campaign. New York must be garrisoned, and pretty strongly too. Long Island must have a considerable Number of men upon it next Summer, or the people of New England will be, making descents and hinder them from bringing off supplies. Gen¹ Howe must leave Brunswic or Amboy fortifyed in his Rear, to retreat to in case of an Accident, or he will forfeit all pretensions to the name of General. These deductions weaken an Army considerably, and so much, that I am of opinion, that if Gen¹. Howe has any reason to expect Reinforcements he will not open the Campaign till they arrive. And I do not think that the Face of Affairs in Europe, looks as if Great Britain could spare more Men towards the reduction of America.

You mistook Gen¹. Washington's meaning in what you refer to. He forbad any of the Military, upon severe penalties, from plundering or appropriating the Effects of what are called Tories, giving as a Reason, that they had nothing to do in the matter. If these people had transgressed the Laws or Regulations of the State in which they live. The Civil power was to judge of that and not the Military. The publication in the N Yk paper respecting the treatment of Doc^r. Brown is a most infamous Falshood. Upon an information ag^t. the Doctor, the General desired he might come up to Morris Town, he came up with no other guard than an Officer, he was here a day or two, but no more a prisoner than I was. He chose to go to New York and did remove with his Effects, some Medecines that he did not carry with him were bought by us. There are some Gentlemen in New York who ought to contradict any Reports of the Generals inhumanity for their families have experienced his Clemency and protection, I will particularly mention. Major Bayard and his Brother, M^r. Apthorp, M^r. O. Delancy and some others, for all last Summer, while they were taking an active part with the Enemy, the General took particular pains to protect their Families and Estates, which never suffered in the least degree. The Constitution and Con-

duct of pennsylvania is what all the World cries out
against. Such Errors must reform themselves. But yet
I think the Gentlemen who were formerly in Office are
somewhat to blame. From the first of this dispute, they
were all backward, and rather discountenanced than gave
any assistance to an opposition, that certainly, in the Eyes
of the warmest friends of Administration was at first war-
rantable. I saw plainly how Matters would go, and that
our provincial Affairs, for want of able pilots, would end
in distraction — I do not think it yet too late to over set
this Cabal, for so it is properly called, but it can only be
done by Men of Sense and Rank stepping forth determined
to give opposition to the power at present hanging over
with undoubted intent to first subjugate and then Rule
with a Rod of Iron. I will write to M^r. Allen by the first
Flag and enquire for Letters. A packet arrived a few
days ago some of the Letters of the 2^d January, that were
sent out open to the General to be forwarded mention the
press for seamen as very hot and all things bearing the
Appearance of War in Europe —

    I am Dear and honoured Sir
      Y^{rs}. most dutifully & Affect^y.
        TENCH TILGHMAN.

   Head Quarters Morris Town 29th March 1777.
Hond. Sir

I last Night had the pleasure of yours of the 20th but
as this happens to be a crowded day of Business I cannot
find time to say as much as I could wish upon the present
public Situation of Affairs. Desertions from the British
Army are daily and numerous. No information can be
got from these people, b⸺t what they see. Genl Howe is
fortifying Brunswic and Amboy strongly and from Appearance seems determined to act upon the defensive till he is
again reinforced. But from the Face of European Affairs

I do not think it probable that a large one can be spared. I am afraid that the Ministry will have so much upon their hands, that East India Affairs will be delayed and that my Brother will remain in suspence. The uncertainty of his Friends keeping their Establishments, was what I always looked upon as the greatest Block in his way — A War with France, which you may depend upon is inevitable, must unhorse the present Ministry and all their Connections. France has been wisely weighing the Value of that Commerce which Eng^d. has madly lost. She has had the ablest Heads and hands at Work to find out the annual exports of European Commodities to America and the Value of the imports of America to Europe. She has been taking means to establish the Manufacture of such Goods as America usually took from Great Britain, and is determined to send out those Goods in their own Bottoms guarded by their own Ships of War. I dont expect to see a declaration of War by France, she will pursue the above Measures and if England can sit tamely by and bear the insult — She is lost indeed — I am sorry that my Sisters should have so seriously taken to heart any expressions in my last letter, I never meant any such thing. I suppose what affected them was, that I desired, if any Accident happened to me that they would share among them some little Matters of Mine by way of Memorial. But by their mode of Reasoning, a Man should never make his Will. I will write to them the first leisure hour and set all to rights again — I wrote to M^r pearce myself and let him know that if he had not purchased a Horse for me, he might let it alone. I will have my Mare up again the latter End of April and send down the Horse I purchased. He is a fine Creature for the Saddle as ever was crossed and will make a fine covering Horse. I imagine M^r pearce will keep him the Season, if he does and you like the Breed, I beg you may send any or all your Mares to him.

I shall have an opportunity of writing to M^r. A. Allen next Wednesday, when I will desire him to inquire for Letters from my Brother upon the arrival of every packet from England.

I am most dutifully & Affect^y Y^{rs}.
Tench Tilghman.

Head Quarters Morris Town 21st April 1777.

Hon^d. Sir

I late last night rec^d yours of the 21st. The Contents really make me exceedingly unhappy as I find myself unable to agree with you in Sentiment upon the present Measures. A Move of the Ships of War and some Transports up the North River and something like a Movement at Amboy and Brunswic towards the same quarter engages the attention of the General and all about him at this time, we shall in a day or two see whether it is real or a diversion, as I expect. I will after that meet you with great pleasure and fix upon a time. I thank you much for the trouble you have been at on account of my Horse, but I have got M^r. Lowery to keep him for me. I wrote to M^r. Pearce by the last post to send my Mare to Philad^a. to Hiltzeimers, who will forward her immediately by one of his Expresses. I will say nothing upon the Score of Politics because it is a subject that ought not at this time to be discussed upon Paper. I wish it might be dropped in all future letters between us, because they may probably fall into other hands than mine. I know your sentiments proceed from a Conviction that present measures are wrong and therefore hurtful to the Country, to the welfare of which I am sure you are at heart a sincere good Wisher, but all will not make the same allowance — I am with unfeigned Affection

y^r. most dutiful Son
Tench Tilghman.

Head Quarters Morris Town 10th May 1777.

Hon^d. Sir

I had the pleasure of yours by Genl Woodford. M^{rs}. Washington sets out for philad^a. in a day or two, if Matters remain as quiet as they are at present I shall attend her so far on her Journey. She is at present a little indisposed, but if she is better, she will set out on Monday. I hope your Business will not oblige you to go to Maryland before I reach Philad^a.

I am y^{rs}. dutifully & affect^y.
TENCH TILGHMAN.

Camp at Middle Brook 10th June 1777.

Hon Sir,

I was much disappointed at finding your letter in Philad^a. instead of yourself. I wrote to you by the post, but you must have missed the Letter. I am afraid I shall be obliged to be in or near Philad^a. soon in a way rather disagreable, as every thing looks like a move of Genl. Howe's Army that Way. We for some time thought that his Views were up the North River, but by a late preparation of Transports both for Horse and Foot, he is certainly going a short Voyage, and Philad^a. I think must be the object — Whether any part of his Army will move by land is uncertain. We have had a vast number of deserters for many days past, they all agree that the whole Army are under orders to hold themselves in readiness to embark, but such orders are sometimes issued to deceive — No reinforcements, except a few recruits, have arrived yet from Europe, and I can hardly think that Genl. Howe, if he expects any, will move before they do arrive. His Army from losses at different times, the sicklyness of his foreign Troops during the Winter, and the natural diminution of all Armies, is considerably reduced. If we should be thrown any time into Philad^a. and you should not be there, I will take care that the House is put into good Hands. I think if my Grandmother is not returned to Maryland she had better do it before a time of hurry and confusion which will certainly happen if the Armies draw that way — Be kind enough to tell M^r. Allen that I delivered his message to the General and that I have made what enquiry I could concerning his son John's having taken a Reg^t. but that I can hear nothing more of it. I am therefore inclined to think that the deserter mistook John Allen for Isaac Allen — Make my affectionate love and regard to my Sisters, and be assured I am

Y^r most dutiful Son
TENCH TILGHMAN.

Camp at Paulius Hill 6th. October 1777.

Hon^d. Sir

I have the pleasure to inform you that I am well after a pretty severe action at Germantown on the 4th. The attack was general, and had not the excessive fogginess of the morning hindered our Wings from knowing of the Success of each other it would have ended in a total defeat of Genl. Howe. When he came into the field he found matters so far against him that orders were given to make Chester the place of Rendezvous in a Retreat. The Attack was made upon two Quarters at day break. The right wing commanded by his Excellency in person entered Germantoun by the way of Chestnut Hill, the first Guard was at Mount Airey, this was carried without much resistance, and the light Infantry and one or two Brigades being posted near, the action soon became severe, we pushed them by degrees from Mount Airey below the lane that leads by the Colledge. A party took post in Cliffdon House and did us considerable mischief from the Windows, the House must be much damaged by our Cannon shot of which a vast number was fired thro' it. Gen¹ Green who commanded our left Wing attacked nearly at the same time that we did, he surprised a Camp near the Market House and drove the Enemy across the town some towards Shippens Common and others down as far as Logans Hill. Had the day been clear everything was in our Hands, but one of our Columns pressing down were mistaken in the fog by part of Gen¹. Greens for the Enemy, while ours mistook his Troops in the same Manner. This unluckily made both halt, and quickly occasioned both to retreat, without any real Cause. The Enemy, taking advantage of the cessation of the pursuit, rallied their men and got up a Reinforcement of the Hessian and British Grenadiers who had been in Philadª. We had brought no more ammunition than the men could carry in their Cartouches and that being nearly expended and the Men fatigued with marching all Night we returned to our Camp. Gen¹. Nash of the North Carolinians was the only Officer of distinction killed. Colº. Stone is wounded in the leg and many other Officers, two of the Generals family are wounded. Mʳ. Lawrens of Carolina slightly and Mʳ. Smith of Virginia his leg broke. The Maryland Regulars bore the brunt of the day, they behaved amazingly well and suffered more in proportion than the others. We are informed the Enemy had one Gen¹. Officer killed and one wounded. Colº. Walcot and Colº Bird it is said were also killed. They attribute their salvation to the Bravery of Lord Cornwallis, who rallied their Men and brought a Reinforcement. Gen¹. Howe was much blamed by the Army, who said they had been amused by him with an account that the Rebel Army was dispersed. We shall be reinforced by near four thousand Men in two or three days from the Northern Army and from Virginia. We shall then try the fortune of another day. Make my thanks to Betsy for her letter which I recᵈ. by Capᵗ. Edmonston and believe me to be Your most dutiful & Affecᵗ. Son,

T. TILGHMAN.

Head Quarters 3ᵈ Decemʳ 1777.

Dear and honoured Sir

Yours by Major Smyth reached me. I do not think there is much probability of Genˡ Howe's leaving Philadᵃ. If he does, his own wants must drive him off. Fortifyed as he is from River to River, four times our Numbers would be insufficient. He has now entirely drawn himself within his line, which extends from the Quarry Hill, thro' your pasture and those grounds, over to Batchelors Hall. They have burned all the Houses in the Vicinity of their lines, beginning with Mʳ. Dickinson's. Mʳ. Penns at Peel Hall has shared the same fate. They have not yet burned the Vine Yard and Mʳ. Merediths but the Windows, Doors and Floors are all taken up. My Aunt Lawrence came out a few day ago and has gone to Northampton. She says Genˡ. Howes behaviour is extremely reserved. Most of the Gentlemen who remained in town, waited upon him. He received them cooly, and has never since taken the least notice of them — I had letters a few days ago from the Govʳ. and Mʳ. Chew, they were both well. I expect Mʳˢ. Penn will come out in a few days, she has the Generals permission; who has very politely offered to permit any intercourse between the Gentlemen and their families that they chuse. Upon my Word from all accounts, They are much happier at the Union than they would have been in Philadᵃ. We have no News except of the Evacuation of Ticonderoga and Mount Independence. As I have wrote to Mʳ. Earle and my Sisters by this conveyance. I have only to assure you that I am

most dutifully and affectʸ yʳˢ

TENCH TILGHMAN.

I was made very happy by receiving a letter from Billy at Middletown in which he informs that he had got Phil from the Fleet.

CORRESPONDENCE.   163

Head Quarters 27th Feby 1778.

Hon^d Sir,

I had the pleasure of receiving yours of the 30th January by Mr S. Chew. That which was intended by M^r. Buchanan came to me by the post, as did your last of the 5th Current. When M^r. Chew returned I was at Trenton on Business. If you want to write to M^r. Shippen send your letter to me and I can forward it by a Flag. You will have seen or heard of M^r. John Allens Death. I imagine M^{rs}. Allen will hardly continue in your house and I therefore think you had better desire M^r. Shippen to get some Gentleman to go into it if M^{rs}. Allen leaves it. It will be a security to it, and prevent its being put to any public use. You ask me if I ever think of my private affairs and what situation they are in? I have the pleasure to inform you that I have taken all possible care of them and that I believe few people's considering the times are in so good. I have collected and secured in good hands about £8000. and for the greatest part of the remainder of our debts have Bonds and real securities. The partnership of F. & T. has only one debt in England something upwards of £1000 Sterling due to the Estate of M^r. Heate which shall be discharged the Moment there is a possibility of remitting money to Europe. Part of the £8000 before mentioned belongs to S. C. & Co. for goods sold upon their account and part of the outstanding debts are likewise upon their accounts. My poor Uncle has indeed suffered cruelly and wantonly by the waste of war. I have not seen him, but he has given me a lively picture of his distress. Till he felt the stroke, he would not, like many others believe, that a British Army could carry desolation with them. He had always by his own Expences and paying my Grandmothers annuity and some other matters, drawn his full proportion of the profits of our Business and I believe, something more. But from the State I have given you

you will perceive, that I have laid up enough to discharge all our Contracts, and if we ever see peaceable times again, enough to make me happy with my own industry. No man can be content with less than I can, and I am confident you will do me the justice to say that none of your Children have made fewer calls upon you than I have done. If any of my Brothers have not hitherto been so fortunate as I have been, I would not even wish that you should deduct from them the extraordinary Expence they have been to you. It will be all the same to me in the end, for they should be welcome sharers to part of whatever I should have, were they to want it — The provision you intend to make for my Sisters is highly pleasing to me. I never could bear the thought of a woman being left in such a situation (if it could be avoided) as to be obliged to accept of an unworthy and disagreable match for want of subsistance. What you have done for Phil shall be most solemnly observed by me, but how ardently I wish that there had never been any occasion for so doing, and that the time may be far off before the trust devolves upon me — His first act was a boyish trick and might have been overlooked. But thank God he has chosen a service that will never throw him in my way as an Enemy — I will endeavour to forward a letter to him, if you send it to me. You will have all the European News in the next weeks Lancaster paper. You may judge of the Complexion of Affairs by the Speech and the subsequent debates. A number of seamen equal to the highest demand last war is called for. Surely this cannot be supposed solely for the American War, because her defence is only by land. The uncommon preparations by France, in the West Indies, cannot be for nothing. She has at least 8000 Men in her Islands. But while she continues to trade with us largely and openly I desire no more. Tho beyond a doubt a french war will in a great measure tend to put a stop to that in America. Lord Campden appears to me to be the only man in England who espouses our Cause from principle. He has sacrificed his interest to his opinion and in that he has been uniform. All the others seem actuated by party Motives and perhaps were they in power would exercise similar Measures. Be pleased to make my compliments to M^r. Earle and tell him when I find a private opportunity I will acknowledge his favors. My Sisters must wait till then also. Let them and my Brothers be assured of my love and be you assured that

I am Y^r. most dutiful & Affect. Son
TENCH TILGHMAN.

Head Quarters Valley Forge, 24 April 1778.
Hon^d. Sir.

I do not know whether the irregularity of the post deprived me of the pleasure of yours of the 18 and 23^d March untill a few days ago, but they did not come to hand before that time. Were I to write you all the news and the amazing change that has lately taken place in the British politics, it would fill a volume. I must refer you to the paper, which I suppose will reach you next week, for the Copy of two intended Acts of parliament sent out by Lord North and his introductory Speech. The impossibility of conquering America is plainly confessed, and because that cannot be effected, terms, giving up everything short of Independency, are at this time of day to be offered. That the former Commissioners had no other powers than those vested in them by the Act of Parliament is now a matter of certainty. This is the last effort to divide. General Howe goes home in a few days and Sir H. Clinton succeeds him. It is said Lord Amherst and General Murray are coming out for the land service and Admiral Keppell for the sea. I cannot say the truth of the last, but we have the first from Genl. Howe himself in the course of a piece of Business which he transacted with Genl. W———n a few days ago relative to an exchange of prisoners — Lord North throws many oblique reflections upon Howes conduct. The letters published under General Washington's signature are not genuine. They are intended for the purposes you mention. He suspects Jack Randolph for the author, as the letters contain a knowledge of his family Affairs that none but a Virginian could be acquainted with — The Sentiments are noble and such as the General himself often expresses. I have heard him declare a thousand times, and he does it every day in the most public Company, that independence was farthest of anything from his thoughts, and that he never entertained the Idea untill he plainly saw that absolute conquest was the aim, and unconditional submission the terms which Great Britain meant to grant — If Ned Tilghman will send his Certificates for Cattle, properly endorsed, to me, I will procure payment for them. He should do it by a safe hand or they may be lost upon the way — I expect a few weeks will throw a vast light upon our Affairs, at present the papers tell all that I know. I shall take a pleasure in giving you the best information.— I began a letter to M^r. Earle the 9th of this Month, and shall continue it till I meet a private opportunity. It will contain abundance of Politics &c. and as I have not much time to spare upon my own account, I shall give you a property in it — I have sent in your letter to M^r. Shippen. I have frequent opportunities of hearing that all our friends in Philad^a are well, and it often lays in my way to do many acts of kindness to those of our acquaintance whom necessity has confined in that City — I am a letter in debt to my Brother James which I will pay him at my leisure — My Sisters are in debt to me, and pray tell them so. However, remember me most affectionately to them and my

Brothers and be assured I am, Your dutiful and Affect. Son

Tench Tilghman.

Head Quarters Valley Forge 31st. May 1778.

Hon^d. Sir

I recd. yours by General Cadwalader and by Genl. Dickinson. I cannot say they gave me pleasure because at the time of writing them you seem to have been under very great uneasiness.— I will not undertake to dictate, but I wish for your own sake, that of your family, and the preservation of your fortune, you would think seriously of conforming to the law of the Country in which you are obliged to live. If you thought the Measures which have been pursued, wrong, you have done everything in your power to oppose them, not by acting, but by speaking your sentiments moderately and in such a manner, that even those of a different opinion have not blamed you. A Majority of people upon this Continent are determined to support the independency of America, and a great European Power has acknowledged and determined also to support them in it. Great Britain has herself in fact acknowledged the independency, for Sir Henry Clinton has this day informed the General that he is charged with dispatches from Lord Howe the Kings Commissioner to Congress. What these dispatches contain I do not know. But formerly they foolishly disdained to mention the name of Congress but in the most contemptuous manner. Things being thus circumstanced, it is no more derogatory to your honour and Conscience to take an Oath of fidelity to the form of Government under which you live, than it is for a Member of any representative Body to take an Oath which he had opposed in the House. He takes it because the Majority think it right — A few days ago M^r. Secretary Matlock inclosed me your parole, and desired me to forward it to you, informing you that you were discharged from it and at liberty to act as you should judge best. I take it for granted that you have seen the law of the State of Pennsylvania which affects you, but lest you should not, I inclose you a single sheet which has the two material sections N°. 8 and 9. As you are out of the province, you may take time to consider well of it, and if you chuse to conform, which I hope in God you will, you may do it any time within ten days after you come in. The folly of the British Ministry in sending out terms after they knew we had concluded an Alliance with France, crowns all their former acts of Madness. The terms of our Alliance with France are generous to the highest degree, we are not even bound to give them an exclusive trade. We only engaged to assist them should they be drawn into a War with England on our Account. You always treated my intelligence of the intentions of france as chimerical. I could not speak plainer than I did consistent with my duty and the confidence which is reposed in me. But you may be assured, that not only France but the whole of her Connection are determined to support America ag^t. Great Britain and whether she will be able to overpower us backed by such powerful Advocates you may judge from the Struggles we have heretofore made alone — The British Army leave Philad^a. in a few days and leave hundreds to curse the wretched Situation into which they are drawn. They must stay exposed to the Resentment of their Countrymen, or go, dependent upon those who care not for them. I do not certainly know who of my former friends intend to remain. Andrew Allen takes his family with him. T. Coxe I am told intends to stay and take his chance. Many have came out and taken the Oaths. M^r. Physick was here to-day and took them. M^r. Chew I am told intends to do the same, but I only have it from report. I do not well understand the Nature of my Brother James's case. If by his parole he is bound to return when called upon, he cannot with any propriety be asked to give any kind of information respecting what he saw while in the hands of the Enemy, either respecting persons or any other Matter. But if his parole was barely to remain at home and not bear Arms during this War, he is only bound to do that. The State have a right to call upon him to give Evidence or to do any other duty in common with other Citizens — These are the rules of Parole in the Army, and I believe what ought to govern every where else — A great quantity of Goods will be left in Philad^a. and there you may supply yourself in a few days. You cannot make use of the mode you propose, I know Officers and others get them out of town but then it is ag^t. orders and if they are found out the Goods are confiscated and the persons punished. Your letter shall be sent in to T. Coxe. Let matters get a little settled and I will engage to bring my rash and childish Brother home in safety provided he will return — surely he will not wish to remain in a Service, in which, void of friends to push his future he may attain a Lieutenancy at the end of his life. His was the inconsiderate action of a Boy and as such I dare say I can get it overlooked, provided he does not persevere till he becomes a Man. I write in haste and incoherently. We are busy in preparing to march to the North River. The British Army goes first to New York, ours of course will be near them — Ten Regiments go to Jamaica — perhaps they may be too late — I shall not be surprised if all the Troops leave the Continent to save the Islands. France has ten thousand Men there ready to strike. I speak not vaguely. I know it as certainly, as I know the Returns of our own Army. You must make my excuses to M^r. Earle, my Sisters and Billy for not writing to them. In fact I have not time. When we are fixed again, you shall hear from me, and have my opinions upon the operations of the Campaign. I imagine at present it will be a quiet one. The British Army in New York will be too strongly posted to attack, and if they detatch to the West Indies they will be too weak to attack us. Adieu my dear and honoured Sir and believe me, your truly Affec^t. Son

TENCH TILGHMAN.

Head Quarters Valley Forge 12th. June 1778.
Hon^d. Sir

You will receive a letter with this, that has been wrote some days, but no opportunity has offered of sending it. The Commissioners have arrived since. They are Earl Carlisle, Govr. Johnstone and M^r. W. Eden. Their Secretary Doc^r. Ferguson. Whether their powers are any greater than expressed in the Acts of parliament I do not know, but I suspect not, from the letters that Govr. Johnstone and M^r. Eden have wrote to the General. They are full of compliment and even adulation, but they regret that they are not likely to have a personal acquaintance with him. Congress you know had, upon the Rec^t. of the Copies of the Acts of Parliament determined not to negociate but upon two Conditions, acknowledgment of Independence, or withdrawing of the Army — I have seen the parliamentary debates to the 10th. of April. Parties were high and very violent. Stocks had fallen to 60 pC^t. and Government was paying from 7 to 9 pc^t. for Money. The Levies intended for America were going to Ireland, or were detained at home for self defence. Invective against the king open and avowed, and the abuse of the Ministry such in both Houses, that nothing but Wretches sunk below contempt, and who are conscious that they have ruined the Nation, could or would bear. It seems agreed on all hands that the American War cannot be supported in conjunction with a french one. The arrival of the Commissioners has postponed the evacuation of Philad^a. a little while, but I imagine it will soon take place. Under the present Situation of Affairs let me again press you to follow a step which several of your friends in similar circumstances to yourself has taken. M^r. Hamilton has taken the Oaths, and Charles Stewart told me to day that M^r. Chew would take them as soon as he came into the Province. He says M^r. Penn only hesitates because he thinks he might involve young M^r. Penn. How this would be in law I do not know. But to see you at peace with and conforming to what is now the establishment of this Country would give me greater pleasure than anything I have experienced in a Contest, in which I have faithfully laboured, and by which I flatter myself I have assisted my friends and have gained some reputation to myself. I am Dear and Hon^d. Sir

Y^r. most dutiful and Affec^t. Son
TENCH TILGHMAN.

Head Quarters Philad^a 22^d June 1778.

Hon^d. Sir

I have been here three days. Every thing is quiet and settled, and I think the sooner you come in the better. M^r. Shippen wishes to see you. The British Army makes very slow marches thro' Jersey. Desertion from them is enormous. Two hundred have come in since yesterday morning and the numbers in Jersey are very great. Genl. Washington has crossed the Delaware with his whole army, and is nearer to Amboy than Genl. Clinton. The whole militia of Jersey are in arms, and I think Genl. Clinton stands a fair chance of sharing the fate of Burgoyne. I must leave town to-morrow or next day and I fear I shall not see you.

I am y^{rs} dutifully and Affec^{ty}.
TENCH TILGHMAN.

Philad^a. 2^d. January 1779

Hon^d Sir

I was much disappointed at finding your letter at this place instead of yourself. Our coming down was a thing of uncertainty and I could not therefore give you notice of it. I shall however have the pleasure of seeing you, for a longer time, and in a more agreeable retired way, as soon as Col°. Harrison returns from Virginia, which will be in February. The moment I heard that Phil was on board the Somerset when she stranded, I wrote to him, and put my letters under cover to Genl. Gates that there might be no miscarriage. I desired him to write to you and to me, and to inform me whether he wanted any assistance in money matters, which I imagine he will not, as the Captains and all the Officers are together, and can have Credit for what they want. I have rec^d. no answer, and am therefore fearful that the letters may have been in a mail from Boston which was taken a little time ago by a set of Villains who infest the mountains in Morris County, and carried into New York. I have the satisfaction to inclose you a letter from my Brother Richard which fortunately reached me just before I left the Camp. I am sincerely glad to find that his prospects are so favourable, and I only hope that his health may be continued. Poor Macrabbie you will see has fallen a Victim to the Climate; Tho' he was always delicate — The October packet has arrived, but no News of any consequence. Parliament were not to meet till the 26 Novem^r. by which time terms of pacification were to be prepared, and the mediating powers I suppose fully sounded. We may expect to hear some thing important from the West Indies in a short time, Count D'Estaing had arrived there and Byron has but lately gone off this coast. If the Count made good use of his time, he had nothing to oppose him by Sea. We shall leave this in a few days for Middle Brook. I sincerely wish you many and happy years being most dutifully & affec^ty y^rs.   TENCH TILGHMAN.

                    Morris Town 12th May 1780.
My dear Will.

I had the pleasure of receiving yours by M^r. Smith, who spent one evening with us, and proceeded the next morning to Elizabeth Town. I was made exceedingly happy by hearing from my Father that Betsey and the Major had at length come to a determination agreeable to them both, and nothing would make a greater addition than being present upon the approaching occasion. But if urgent Business did not really intervene, I could not consistent with my reputation leave the Army at a time when something active may be expected — My Heart will be with you and that must suffice — I am not without hopes that I may keep a merry Christmas with you — I shall however expect a minute account from you of the operations of the wedding Week — Alas poor Polly! Hamilton is a gone man, and I am too old for his substitute — She had better look out for herself and not put her trust in Man. She need not be jealous of the little Saint — She is gone to Pennsylvania and has no other impressions than those of regard for a very pretty good tempered Girl, the daughter of one of my most valuable acquaintances. The Marquis de la Fayette has made us a most unexpected but Welcome Visit. He left france the 20th March — Matters were perfectly quiet among the great Continental powers in Europe except those already engaged in the War. Holland determined upon a neutrality, and the Emperor and King of prussia who hold the Balance determined not to suffer any interference — I have luckily just heard of M^r. Witherstandt who does not allow me a moment more than to say I am

                       Y^r. most Affect. Brother
                                TENCH TILGHMAN.

(Letter addressed to Mr. William Tilghman at Chester Town Md.)

Head Quarters New Windsor, 12th June 1781.
My dear William

I have rec^d. yours of the 4th. of June, which has been in good measure answered by My other letter herewith — The second letter which you appear to have written has not reached. I have given you my reasons why I would wish you to defer your Voyage, " till you see what will become of the expected Negociation in Europe. It gives me pain to tell you that I cannot, Without subjecting myself to censure, interfere in the least, in procuring your recommendations to go to England by the way of France or Holland. I am placed in as delicate a situation as it is possible for a Man to be. I am, from my station, Master of the most valuable Secrets of the Cabinet and the Field, and it might give cause of umbrage and suspicion were I, at this critical Moment, to interest myself in procuring the passage of a Brother to England. Tho' I may know his intentions are perfectly innocent, others may not or will not. You cannot conceive how many attempts have been made, some time ago, to alarm the Generals suspicions, as to my being near his person — Thank God — He has been too generous to listen to them — and the many proofs I have given of my attachment have silenced every malignant whisper of the kind. As I never have given the least handle for censure, I am determined never to do it — Nothing will give me so much satisfaction as to hear that you defer your resolution for the present — If you still persist, you have the kindest wishes of

Y^r. most affectionate Brother
TENCH TILGHMAN.

M^r. William Tilghman Jr.
    Chester Town
        Maryland.

New Windsor 10th : June 1781.

My dear Brother,

I had not the pleasure of receiving your letter of the 27th : of April untill three days past. What you mention is out of General Washingtons power to grant — all permits for Citizens to go within the lines of the enemy or beyond sea must be obtained from the Civil Authority of the State within which they reside — perhaps this may not reach you before you may have proceeded too far to recede — I mean as to having engaged a passage to Europe from Philadª. If you have not and will take my advice you will defer the matter 'till next Spring — There is the strongest probability that you will be able to put your resolution in execution then in a manner which can bring no reflexion upon your Connections or be of any future disadvantage to you — For you know very well that all are looked upon with Suspicion and jealousy who leave America to go to England and you also know that severe penal laws have been passed which affect the Estates of such persons. If then by waiting a few months you have a chance of avoiding both inconveniences I think you will do well to make the trial — The foundation of a peace is laid, and as Great Britain must by this time see that she cannot effect the conquest of this Country and that all the maritime powers of Europe are determined that she shall not, I imagine the mediating princes will not find much difficulty in bringing the contending parties to terms — Having been obliged to put off my visit in the Spring I cannot now think of it 'till the Campaign is over — If I survive it nothing shall prevent my seeing you all as soon as the Army goes into Quarters. I write to my Father and the Girls you have therefore only to make my Compliments to all our Friends and acquaintance, and to forward the inclosed to M^r. Chew and M^r. Hall by the first opportunities.

I am your very Affectionate Brother
TENCH TILGHMAN.

do tell our Brother the Major that as he is my junior Officer and a Man of more leisure than I am, I command him to open a correspondence with me.

M^r. Willm. Tilghman jun^r.
    Chestertown M^d.

RENEWALS 458-4574

DATE DUE

OCT 29			
GAYLORD			PRINTED IN U.S.A